TIME

SPECIAL EDITION

The Science of Childhood

Inside the Minds of
Our Younger Selves

Contents

Parts of this edition were previously published by TIME and Real Simple.

Introduction

THE BIRTH OF A NEW BABY OFFERS A
CHANCE TO PONDER THE MYSTERY—AND
THE MAGIC—OF CHILDHOOD

BY BRYAN WALSH

s I write these words, my wife and I are just a few weeks away from the birth of our first child, a boy. The birth will be the culmination of months of waiting and hoping, anxiety and excitement. If all goes well, we'll take him home from the hospital after a couple of days. I will drive more carefully than I have ever driven before, and we'll walk up the stairs to our apartment, finally ready to meet this alien who has come into our lives.

I mean alien in the most loving way possible! But what else should I call a wriggling little person who can't talk or walk, who sees the world through eyes that are utterly unlike mine? All adults have this in common—we've all gone through childhood. But it is almost impossible to remember what it was like to walk through the door on our first day of school, and to feel it as we felt it then, not as an adult recalling stray details. Childhood leaves its marks on all of us, some deeper than others, but for adults it is a foreign, if vaguely recognizable, country.

That's because, contrary to what was once assumed, children are not simply small, irrational versions of their parents, waiting to be shaped and socialized into grown-ups. As the developmental psychologist Alison Gopnik writes, children "learn more, imagine more, care more and experience more than we would have ever thought possible." Young children can't read or write, but they have extraordinary imaginations as well as a profound sense of morality. If at times parents lament that they can't understand their children, they shouldn't be surprised. Children are inquisitive visitors in the adult world. Or perhaps adults are visitors in theirs.

All of which can make a first-time parent-to-be a bit nervous—or more nervous. It's not just that my wife and I will be responsible for keeping him alive 24 hours a day, from the moment we bring him home. We'll also need to learn to meet our son on his level and, as much as possible, see the world through his eyes. And that will require more than getting down on the floor with him.

There are benefits in becoming fluent in the language of children—and not just the baby sign language you can learn from William Paul White and Kathleen Ann Harper in this book. Gopnik calls babies and young children the "R&D division of the human species," and by observing how children learn about the world, we can learn about what it means to be human. Our childhood isn't just the beginning of life but also its foundation, and it may be what sets us apart from our closest animal relatives.

There's no going back to being a child, but being a parent is the next closest thing. We've become a culture of parents, obsessed over how to raise our children, warring over our strategies. And so we should—being a parent will be the most important job most of us will ever have, and you'll find stories in this book to help you at every stage of your child's life. Yet in focusing on parenting, we sometimes risk losing sight of the children and the extraordinary adventure they live each day.

I can't wait to meet my son, and I can't wait to see who he turns out to be. But I know he'll be an explorer, as all children are, charting a fresh path through the world. And though I may appear to be leading, it will be his footsteps I'll be following.

CHAPTER ONE

Babies

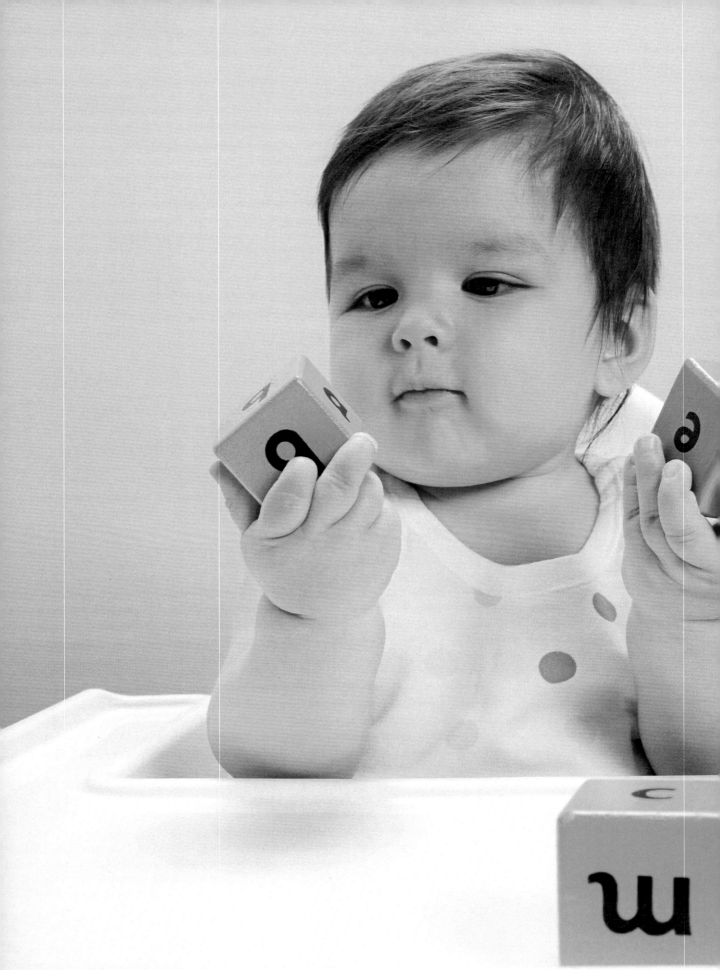

The Start of Thinking

UNDERSTANDING HOW
CHILDREN DEVELOP WILL
HELP US UNDERSTAND
OURSELVES

BY ALISON GOPNIK

Childhood is a profound part of the human condition. But we almost always think about it in individual first-person terms: What should I do, now, about my child? Most books about children are like this—memoirs and novels, the ubiquitous parenting advice books. But childhood is not just a particular plot complication of Irish autobiographies or a particular problem to be solved by American self-help programs. It is not even just something that all human beings share. New science tells us that childhood is a big part of what makes all human beings human.

Children are, at once, deeply familiar and profoundly alien. Sometimes we feel that they are just like us—and sometimes they seem to live in a completely different world. Their minds seem drastically limited; they know so much less than we do. And yet long before

they can read or write, they have extraordinary powers of imagination and creativity, and long before they go to school, they have remarkable learning abilities.

The younger children are, the more mysterious they are. New scientific research has both illuminated and deepened the mystery. In the past 40 years, there's been a revolution in our scientific understanding of babies and young children. We used to think that babies and young children were irrational, egocentric and amoral. Their thinking and experience were concrete, immediate and limited. In fact, psychologists and neuroscientists have discovered that babies not only know more and learn more but also imagine more and experience more than we would ever have thought. In some ways, young children are actually smarter, more imaginative and maybe even more conscious than adults.

Why do we have a period of childhood at all? Childhood plays a special role in human evolution. Imagine an evolutionary biolo-

Young children are actually smarter, more imaginative and maybe even more conscious than adults.

gist from Alpha Centauri who visited Earth 150,000 years ago and was trying to decide what distinguished *Homo sapiens* from their other primate relatives. What would leap out at her would be our distinctive "life history," as biologists say. Human beings have a much more extended period of immaturity and dependence, a much longer childhood, than other species. Chimp babies produce as much food as they consume by the time they are 7; even in hunter-gatherer cultures, human children don't pull their own weight till they're at least 15.

Humans also have always had to invest in taking care of those children. Unlike among

our closest primate relatives, human fathers, grandmothers and "alloparents"—unrelated adults—all help take care of those needy young. Why make babies so helpless for so long, and why make adults invest so much time and energy in caring for them?

This protracted period of immaturity is intimately tied up with capacities for imagination and learning. Across hundreds of different species of animals, there is a very general correlation between the length of childhood and relative brain size and intelligence. Humans have the longest childhood, the largest brains and the greatest capacities for learning and imagination. The major evolutionary advantage of human beings is our ability to escape from the constraints of evolution. We can learn about our environment, we can imagine different environments, and we can turn those imagined environments into reality. And as we are an intensely social species, other people are the most important part of our environment. We are particularly likely

to learn about people and to use that knowledge to change the way other people behave and the way we ourselves behave. The result is that human beings—as a central part of our evolutionary endowment and as the deepest part of our human nature—are engaged in a constant cycle of change. We change our surroundings, and our surroundings change us. We alter other people's behavior, and their behavior alters ours.

We begin life with the capacity to learn more effectively and more flexibly about our environment than any other species. This knowledge lets us imagine new environments, even radically new environments, and act to change the existing ones. Then we can learn about the unexpected features of the new environment that we have created, change that environment once again, and so on. What neuroscientists call plasticity—the ability to change in light of experience—is the key to human nature at every level from brains to minds to societies.

As crucial as learning is to the process, the human capacity for change goes beyond it. Learning is about the way the world changes our mind. But our mind can also change the world. Developing a new theory about the world allows us to imagine other ways the world might be. Understanding other people and ourselves lets us imagine new ways of being human. At the same time, to change our world, ourselves and our society, we have to think about what we *ought* to be like, as well as what we actually are like.

These capacities have great advantages; they allow us to adapt to more different environments than any other species and to change our own environments in a way that no other animal can. But they also have one great disadvantage: learning takes time. You don't want to be stuck exploring all the new possible ways to hunt deer when you haven't eaten for two days, or learning all the accumulated cultural wisdom about saber-toothed tigers when one is chasing you. What's more, computer scientists and neuroscientists have identified a basic trade-off between exploring and exploiting, learning and acting. The very same things that make adult humans effective at planning and acting—focus, control and the ability to ignore distractions—can make them less effective at picking up lots of new information and creatively imagining new possibilities.

An animal that depends on imagination has to have some time to exercise it. Childhood is that time. Literally, children are designed for learning. When we're children, we're devoted to learning about our world and imagining all the other ways that world could be. When we become adults, we put all that we've learned and imagined to use.

There's a kind of evolutionary division of labor between children and adults. Children are the R&D department of the human species—the blue-sky guys, the ones who brainstorm. Adults are production and marketing. Children make the discoveries, and we implement them. They think up a million new ideas, mostly useless, and we take the three or four good ones and make them real. Children aren't just primitive grown-ups gradually at-taining our perfection and complexity. Instead, children and adults are different forms of *Homo sapiens*. They have very different brains—though equally complex and powerful—and those different minds are designed to serve different evolutionary functions. Human development is more like metamorphosis, like caterpillars becoming butterflies, than like simple growth—though it may seem that the children are the vibrant, wandering butterflies who transform into the caterpillars inching along the grown-up path.

If we focus only on the adult abilities of long-term planning and swift and automatic execution, then babies and young children will indeed look pretty pathetic. But if we focus on our distinctive capacities for change, then it's the adults who look slow. The caterpillars and butterflies do different things well.

Psychologists, philosophers, neuroscientists and computer scientists are beginning to carefully and precisely identify some of the underlying mechanisms that give us this distinctly human capacity for change—the aspects of our nature that allow nurture and culture to take place. We are even starting to develop rigorous mathematical accounts of some of those mechanisms. This new research and thinking has given us a new understanding of how the biological computers in our skulls produce human freedom and flexibility.

The basic evolutionary division of labor between children and adults is reflected in their minds, their brains and their everyday activities. Just in the past few years, dozens of studies have shown that even the youngest babies, much like scientists, can learn from statistical patterns and rapidly use evidence to draw causal conclusions about the world. Psychologists have shown that babies and young children unconsciously use the same powerful learning techniques, called Bayesian modeling, that have been adopted in much of machine learning and artificial intelligence.

In fact, in my lab at the University of California, Berkeley, where I study developmental psychology, we have shown that preschoolers can be more creative learners than adults are. For example, in one experiment, we show adults and 4-year-olds evidence that a machine works in an obvious way or a more

How Culture Shapes Infant Attitude

U.S. PARENTS DISCOURAGE THEIR BABIES FROM SHOWING NEGATIVITY

BY BELINDA LUSCOMBE

Babies born in the United States are more social and impulsive than those from some other countries, a 2016 study found. They're also, according to their moms, more likely to enjoy highly stimulating activities, less likely to be unhappy or angry, and easier to comfort when they do get upset.

Researchers from three countries compared kids from the U.S. with those from Chile, South Korea and Poland. They found that kids from Chile were the most active and more prone to have trouble concentrating on one task for an extended period. Their temperamental opposite, the study found, were the South Koreans, who were more likely to have long attention spans and less need to run around. They were also the most cuddly. Polish babies were more prone to exhibit melancholy and took longer to comfort when upset than their foreign cousins.

The study, which was published in the *European Journal of Developmental Psychology*, used questionnaires about kids' behavior co-designed by one of the authors, Maria Gartstein, and filled out by mothers. The questionnaire asked how often babies displayed almost 200 different behaviors at certain ages. The researchers then categorized those behaviors into 14 different characteristics ranging from cuddliness to vocal reactivity.

The new research builds on a former study that examined the differences between (calmer and happier) Dutch and (more stimulated and easily frustrated) American babies.

If it seems as if the infants' traits fulfill a certain set of stereotypes, it's not your imagination. Gartstein, who is a psychologist at Washington State University, is testing the theory that toddlers' temperaments are very influenced by their parents' values. Research has shown, for instance, that American society is not highly tolerant of negativity, which may mean American parents are discouraging their kids from expressing negative emotions.

Likewise, it's possible, Gartstein suggests, that Polish infants may be responding to their culture's willingness to talk about emotions and feelings. "It works to be [more active] in the Chilean context because mothers are more attentive," says Gartstein. "It makes sense."

Why study cultural differences in toddlers? "The vast majority of psychological literature is based in the West," says Gartstein. "There is a question as to what extent [our findings] are universal." Differences in temperament, which is considered to be the foundation of personality, may illuminate what parts of personality or mood disorders may be the result of context. It may help to explain why, for example, American kids have far higher rates of attention deficit disorder than kids from other countries.

"This gives us an opportunity to look at the differences that emerge when you have these vastly different approaches among parents," says Gartstein, "and what they believe are the critical pieces that lead to kids' happiness and success."

unexpected one. Children are more likely to discover the unexpected option that fits the data, while adults stick with the ideas they had before and ignore the new evidence. We've found something similar in the social world. We showed adults and children different patterns of interaction between different people who played with different toys. Then we asked the participants to explain why the characters acted as they did—for example, why someone played with a risky toy or avoided it. Children were more likely than adults to use the data to make up new hypotheses instead of relying on the assumptions they started with.

Babies' brains also seem to have special qualities that make them especially well-suited for imagination and learning. Babies' brains are actually more highly connected than adult brains; more neural pathways are available to babies than to adults. As we grow older and experience more, our brains "prune out" the weaker, less used pathways and strengthen the ones that are used more often. If you were to look at a map of a baby's brain, it would look like old Paris, with lots of winding, interconnected little streets. In the adult brain, those little streets have been replaced by fewer but more efficient neural boulevards, capable of much more traffic. Young brains are also much more plastic and flexible—they change much more easily. But they are much less efficient; they don't work as quickly or effectively.

There are even more specific brain changes that play a particularly important role in the metamorphosis from childhood to adulthood. They involve the prefrontal cortex, a part of the brain that is uniquely well-developed in human beings and that neuroscientists often argue is the seat of distinctly human abilities for thinking, planning and control. The prefrontal cortex is one of the last parts of the brain to mature. It continues to change through adolescence and beyond.

You might think this means that children are defective adults, that they lack the parts of the brain that are most crucial for rational adult thought. But you could equally say that, when it comes to imagination and learning, prefrontal immaturity allows children to be super-adults. The prefrontal cortex is espe-

Young brains are much more plastic and flexible—they change much more easily. But they are much less efficient; they don't work as quickly or effectively.

sider as many possibilities as you can, even wild and unprecedented ones. In learning, you want to remain open to all the possibilities, even unlikely ones, that may turn out to be the truth. And studies show that, in adults, less control activity of the frontal areas can lead to more creativity and better learning. The lack of strong prefrontal control may actually be a benefit of childhood. In fact, there is some evidence that high IQ is correlated with later maturing and more plastic frontal lobes. Keeping your mind open longer may be part of what makes you smarter.

Those different brains and minds mean that adults and children also spend their days differently—we work; children play. Play is the signature of childhood. It's a living, visible manifestation of imagination and learning in action. It's also the most visible sign of the paradoxically useful uselessness of immaturity. People have long thought intuitively that play was important for children. But we've only recently begun to show this scientifically. New studies of "active learning" show that preschoolers prefer to play with the objects that will teach them the most, and they spontaneously play in ways that let them learn the most about how those objects work. Their vividly imaginative, pretend play is related to their ability to think "counterfactually"—to imagine other ways that the world could be—and their ability to figure out how people work.

More than any other creature, human beings are able to change. We change the world around us, other people and ourselves. Nurture is our nature, and culture is our most important and fundamental instinct. And the fact that we change explains why children are the way they are—and even why childhood exists at all. Studying children, and childhood, is the best way to explain how our distinctive human abilities for change emerge. Understanding children lets us understand our human ability to learn about new worlds—and even create them.

cially involved in the act of "inhibition." It actually helps shut down other parts of the brain, limiting and focusing experience, action and thought. This process is crucial for the complex thinking, planning and acting that adults engage in. To execute a complex plan, for example, you have to perform just the actions that are dictated by that plan and not all the other possible actions. And you have to pay attention to just the events that are relevant to your plan and not all the others.

But inhibition has a downside if you are primarily interested in imagination and learning. To be imaginative, you want to con-

Excerpts adapted by the author from *The Philosophical Baby*, by Alison Gopnik. Copyright © 2009 by Alison Gopnik. Jacket design by Charlotte Strick. Jacket photograph © Tatjana Alvegård. Reprinted by permission of Farrar, Straus and Giroux.

Signs of a Happy Baby

LEARN TO SPEAK TO YOUR
CHILD WITHOUT WORDS
THROUGH A LESSON IN
INFANT SIGN LANGUAGE

BY WILLIAM PAUL WHITE AND
KATHLEEN ANN HARPER

 Your baby understands more than you probably realize. Research shows that babies as young as six months can identify objects like an apple, a banana and the location of the arm on a picture of a body. Another study showed that children at 16 months could speak an average of only 40 words but could comprehend up to eight times that number. Yet babies don't have large enough vocabularies to express their thoughts and desires verbally until a language burst that occurs around 18 months or later.

Eighteen months is a long time to know what you want to say, have ideas you'd like to share but have minimal tools to express yourself with the people around you. Baby sign language uses gestures for communication to

More

Put your fingertips and thumbs together, creating the shape of a flattened O with each hand. Tap the fingertips of the hands together twice, like you're bringing an item in one hand toward more of the item held in the other.
Use this sign at mealtime, playtime or story time by offering a little bit of food, a short period of activity or a few pages of a story and then asking, "Do you want more?" as you sign the word "more."

All Done / Finished

Hold both of your hands in front of you at chest height, palms facing in and fingers spread apart.
Flip the hands by twisting your wrists, ending with both palms facing away from you like you're brushing something away.
The sign can be used along with the question "Are you all done?" If the answer appears to be yes, respond appropriately by clearing away the remainder of the meal or shifting to another activity.

Baby

Create a cradle with your arms placed one on top of the other and your palms facing up. Gently swing your arms from side to side like you're rocking a baby. Small children are often fascinated by other babies, so you can point out babies you see at the park or at the store while saying and signing "baby."

bridge that gap, reducing frustration for children and parents alike.

Jeannie Rosenthal started signing when her daughter, Lillian, was six months old. "I'm glad to have this brilliant skill that helps us have so much fun getting to know Lilly through signs," says Jeannie. "At 15 months, she has about 60 words—around 45 signs and 15 spoken words. Her range of communication—understanding and expression—is really wide."

When you sign with your baby, you take advantage of the natural human tendency to communicate with the whole body, not only with spoken words but with facial expressions and body language too. With signing, you can know for sure what your child wants to eat, discover what interests your baby, and gain a better understanding of why your child is crying, so you can do something about it.

"My daughter was cranky and we didn't know what was going on," remembers Yunting Dai, mom to Elisabeth. "We took her to see the pediatrician, telling him that she signed pain at her ear. They found out that

Mommy/Mother

Hold your dominant hand in front of your face with your thumb resting on your chin, fingers facing up and spread apart. Tap the thumb twice against your chin. If you're the child's mother, point to yourself and sign and say "Mommy." If you're another caregiver, you can say, "There's Mommy!" as you point to the mom while signing "Mommy."

Daddy/Father

With the thumb of your dominant hand resting on your forehead and your fingers splayed and pointing up, tap the thumb of your dominant hand twice against your forehead. Say "There's Daddy!" as you point to Daddy and sign "Daddy." If you're the dad, point to yourself and say and sign "Daddy."

Cat

With each hand, place your thumb and index finger together to form an *O* shape while keeping the other fingers pointing up. Put your thumbs and index fingers on either side of your mouth and move them outward from your cheeks with a double movement, like you're showing the position of a cat's whiskers. If you have something in your hand, it's OK to do signs that normally use two hands with one.

day that she had an ear infection."

You can start signing with your baby at any time, but an ideal age to begin is when your child is six to eight months old. At this age, children's long-term memories are developmentally ready to retain the words they hear and the signs they see. Babies also start developing the motor skills and hand-eye coordination to make more precise gestures at this time. It's never too late to get benefits from signing: preschoolers are less aggressive when there's signing in the classroom, and elementary-school-age kids build bigger vo-cabularies and score higher on spelling tests after learning how to fingerspell the alphabet.

Contrary to some parents' fears, using sign language with your child won't slow verbal language development. Research studies have shown that signing with your baby has a positive impact on the brain, including accelerating verbal language skills. The use of sign language enhances what researchers call "joint attention," which is when people use gazes and gestures to bring their common focus to an object or activity. In one study, parents and children who signed were more likely to en-

Milk

Hold your hand at chest level in the shape of the letter *C*. Open and close your fist several times to represent the action of milking a cow. Use this sign in context when you're feeding your child milk, either by breastfeeding or from a bottle or sippy cup.

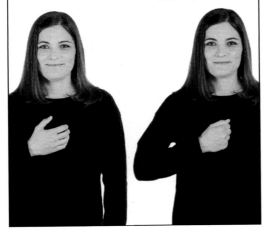

gage in joint attention activities than those who didn't know how to sign. Baby sign language gives preverbal children a way to initiate joint attention and start conversations about topics that interest them. When parents verbalize the signs and continue the dialogue, children's expanding vocabularies flourish.

Children learn sign language best in an immersive environment, just like they learn spoken language by being immersed in the sounds of speech all the time. To build your child's vocabulary, speak verbally and sign as much as you can, making connections between the object or activity, the spoken word and the sign. Receptive language begins before expressive language—and expressive language skills aren't an indicator of comprehension, so don't wait for your child to sign back before teaching additional signs. You can't overload your child's brain; your baby is hungry for lots of information, and there is room for it all.

Adapted from *Signs of a Happy Baby: The Baby Sign Language Book*, by William Paul White and Kathleen Ann Harper. © 2017 Morgan James Publishing. For more information, visit happybabysigns.com.

How Toddlers Learn to Speak

THE NATIONAL LANGUAGE PARENTS SPEAK AFFECTS HOW CHILDREN PICK UP WORDS

BY JEFFREY KLUGER

Whether you know it or not, at some point in your life you've larped a balloon. You've also larped your hand, a flag and a baseball bat. Larping, in the world of nonsense words, means waving—at least in one small corner of academia—and that, it turns out, has helped reveal a lot about how children learn language in general, and how to help kids with language impairments in particular.

Among the more than 6,500 languages in the world, there are innumerable differences in grammar, tone, inflection and more. One of the less appreciated differences concerns the relative balance between nouns and verbs. English and other European languages tend to favor nouns a bit. Languages like Korean, Japanese and Hindi go the other way, with Korean speakers using about six verbs to every four nouns.

To determine how this affects the way children come to master their native tongues, professor of psychology Sandra Waxman of Northwestern University and Sudha Arunachalam, an assistant professor of speech and hearing sciences at Boston University, collaborated with a team of investigators in Korea for a study published in *Linguistic Acquisition: A Journal of Developmental Linguistics*. In both labs on both sides of the world, small sample groups of 24-month-old children were shown a series of videos of people engaged in simple actions. An adult would describe what was going on as the kids watched but would use an invented word in place of the verb. In the case of a person waving a balloon, the description was "The girl is larping the balloon." In Korea, an equally meaningless word was used in an otherwise correct sentence. The children were then shown two more side-by-side videos: in one, a child was waving a spoon; in the other, a child was bouncing a balloon.

"We preserve the action but use a new object in one case," says Arunachalam, "and we preserve the object but with a new action in the other." The kids were then all asked the same question—"Show me larping"—in English or Korean. Their answers differed dramatically, and their native language seemed to be responsible.

The natural assumption would be that the Korean toddlers, growing up with a language that gives primacy to verbs, would do better on the test since they would be likelier

The English language tends to favor nouns. Languages like Korean, Japanese and Hindi go the other way.

to be more sensitive to activities than to objects. But in fact the opposite was true: the English speakers were likelier to ignore the balloon in the second trial and correctly pay attention to the waving, while the Korean toddlers were more drawn to the balloon. The explanation, the investigators believe, was in the way the original statement, "The girl is larping the balloon," was phrased.

"In Korean, nouns tend to be dropped from sentences," says Arunachalam. "So a child would typically be told simply, 'The girl is larping,' and figure out the rest. When you add the noun, Korean babies get overwhelmed, so they just latch onto something they recognize, which is the balloon." The best way to improve the Korean children's performance was to prime them differently, dropping not just the object of the sentence (the balloon) but also the subject (the girl). A lean, quick declarative like "Oh, look, larping!" left no room for confusion.

The inevitable question, of course, is so what? This kind of scenario is not one that typically comes up in children's lives, and if you're teaching your babies nonsense verbs, perhaps you shouldn't be teaching them at all. But not all kids learn to speak equally well, and for those who are having challenges—especially those who require some kind of remedial education—it can make a very big difference to know exactly how their native tongue conditions them to learn.

"There are a lot of programs that teach you how to talk to a child," says Arunachalam, "and those can differ from language to language." Human beings may have 6,500 different ways to talk among themselves, but learning disabilities are universal. Knowing how any one child masters speech can help make recovery universal too.

Getting Back on Track

SOMETIMES EVEN GOOD KIDS BREAK A LITTLE BAD.
HERE'S HOW TO HELP YOURSELF HELP THEM

BY INGELA RATLEDGE

 nce you made it through those sleepless nights with an infant and your child responded to language, it seemed most problems could be tackled with a stern "no"—or maybe three. But even kids who initially follow every rule can eventually start veering off course. Suddenly a child who loved green beans refuses anything but waffle fries. To help you straighten out those wayward souls, we talked to moms who have done it and then consulted experts to find out why these women's solutions were successful. So no matter which path your kids choose, you can keep them moving in the right direction.

"My child started throwing tantrums to get what he wanted."
—Rachel O'Connell, Ashland, Mass.

The Problem: A 2-year-old who learned that a screaming fit usually resulted in a toy. "My son would let loose these truly bloodcurdling screams that would go on until one of us would give him whatever it took to make that awful noise stop," says O'Connell. "One day he screamed so much he lost his voice."

The Fix: A nifty disappearing act. As soon as her son launched into one of his fits, O'Connell and her husband would calmly and promptly remove themselves from the action. "We'd go into another room right away, but we'd tell him he could come find us when he was finished," she says. "Knowing that we weren't going to get riled up or be around did the trick eventually. Within a week, the screaming sessions were down to less than a minute."

The Expert Take: "When you say, 'I'm not going to stay in the room with you for this,' it's removing attention from the tantrum, which says, 'This is not acceptable,'" says Rex Forehand, a professor of psychology at the University of Vermont and a co-author of *Parenting the Strong-Willed Child*. "Toddlers might erupt like Mount Vesuvius, but then they have to vent and let go of upset feelings," says Robert A. MacKenzie, a family therapist and the author of the *Setting Limits* book series. Stuck in Target? You can't leave a screaming child in housewares. Forehand suggests picking up the child, leaving the store and putting him in the backseat of the car—alone—while you stand outside with the keys. Wait a few minutes; if the tantrum stops, let him out and go back inside.

"It took two hours to put my child to bed."

—Kerri Eastham, Torrance, Calif.

The Problem: A bedtime process that dragged on into the wee hours. Eastham's 2½-year-old daughter had, over time, become a master of delaying bedtime. "Some requests were legitimate, like 'One more trip to the bathroom.' Others were ridiculous: 'One more dinner, please?' " says Eastham.

The Fix: A photo-driven bedtime routine. "I took pictures of my daughter brushing her teeth, washing her face and so on. We laminated them and taped them in order to a strip of paper. When each one was completed, she would say, 'Check!' " says Eastham. "And if she asked for another drink of water, I'd show her the chart and say, 'See? We already did that.' It worked right away."

The Expert Take: "Kids love clarity—they crave it," says MacKenzie. "An approach like this answers all the questions: What's next? How far can I go? How much is left?" To keep the novelty of the chart from wearing off, MacKenzie recommends updating it from time to time—which Eastham has done by subbing in new pictures (showing off new teeth or new pink pajamas) and adding in stickers that function as check marks (and peel off easily from the laminated photos).

"My kids rushed through dinner just to get to dessert."

—Gia Blount, Pasadena, Calif.

The Problem: Using dessert as a reward for eating well eventually turned dinner into an afterthought. "My two boys would rush through dinner and eat the bare minimum to earn their 'reward.' There were constant negotiations and power struggles," says Blount.

The Fix: Blount began to serve dinner family-style, with all the dishes—even dessert—presented at once. The boys were expected to serve themselves and make their own choices without any intervention from their parents. "The first night, my younger one grabbed a cookie and inhaled it. But then he relaxed and ate a complete meal," says Blount. Eventually she began phasing out dessert at every meal—without protests.

The Expert Take: "It's important to stop distinguishing between 'good' and 'bad' foods," says Adele Faber, a co-author of *How to Talk So Kids Will Listen & Listen So Kids Will Talk*. "Making food attractive, like arranging peas in the shape of a smiley face or cutting fruit into shapes, will make kids more likely to eat it." Considering dessert as a part of the meal, rather than as an overvalued treat, eliminates it as a bargaining chip. And if your child does eat six cookies before serving himself any spinach, consider this: "In studies, when kids were allowed to eat whatever they wanted, they just ate dessert at first. But within a few weeks, they were back to a balanced meal," says Kevin Leman, a psychologist and the author of *Have a New Kid by Friday*.

"My child was obsessed with TV."

—Elizabeth Williams, Hoboken, N.J.

The Problem: A spiraling screen-time habit. (Any parent who's dared to shut off *Octonauts* or *Paw Patrol* after just one episode—and faced the subsequent wrath—can surely relate.) "Our 4-year-old son became obsessed and wanted to watch constantly," says Williams.

The Fix: Williams didn't want her family to spend their waking hours glued to the tube or have television be the go-to source of entertainment, so she banned it during the week—for Mom and Dad too. "Exceptions are made for presidential debates and speeches and baseball opening day," she says. "It was clear-cut, and the rule applied fairly to everybody." Williams subbed in plenty of card games (Uno was a favorite), kitchen science experiments and fun, drill-style challenges. "I would say, 'How long will it take you to walk backwards around the apartment three times? I'll time you!' He loved being timed," she says.

The Expert Take: "The idea of limiting [screen] time is great, but whether you need to cut it out altogether is up to you," says Forehand. Even if you do allow your kids to watch during the week, there are ways to diversify the subject. Use your child's interest in particular programs to create an educational experience. "Say, 'Oh, you're interested in ducks?

Let's learn more about them. We can go to the library and find books that tell us what they do,' " suggests Faber.

"My daughter went berserk when we left her with a babysitter."
—Jan Schwieters, Eden Prairie, Minn.

The Problem: Temper tantrums at the sight of a sitter. "Our 3-year-old became hysterical when we left her with someone else. We would hand over a screaming toddler and bolt. It was terrible," says Schwieters.

The Fix: An earlier arrival and special activities. "If we were leaving at 7, I'd have the sitter come at 6:40 and set them up for a popcorn party or outside playtime," says Schwieters. Her daughter felt secure enough to get fully engaged in the thing she was doing, since Mom and Dad were still home, and she barely batted an eye when they left.

The Expert Take: "This is an excellent solution for three reasons," says Forehand. "It takes the stress out of the parents' leaving, it gives the child the opportunity to see that being with a sitter is fun, and it creates a distraction." To make the tactic even more successful, "have fun activities that are reserved for times when the sitter is there," says Nicholas Long, a professor of pediatrics at the University of Arkansas for Medical Sciences and the co-author with Forehand of *Parenting the Strong-Willed Child*. Make up a new cookie recipe (Babysitter Butterscotch Bombs!) or let them build a fort your child can sleep in.

"My daughter's room was a disaster site."
—Michelle LeMasurier, Duluth, Minn.

The Problem: A formerly neat 14-year-old whose bedroom slowly morphed into a landfill look-alike. "At its worst, you couldn't see the floor," says LeMasurier.

The Fix: Top Secret Operation Heave-Ho.

LeMasurier bagged all her daughter's out-of-place belongings (clothes, books, papers, toiletries) and moved them to the garage while she was out one afternoon. "Wow, did that get her attention," LeMasurier says. To get the items back, her daughter had to reorganize. "We reworked her closet area—she helped design it—and she arranged things the way she wanted to keep them in the future," says LeMasurier. The result? Her daughter had a room she could be proud of—and a reason to keep it spick-and-span.

The Expert Take: "Shock value definitely works," says Leman. "Older kids don't like their stuff touched." The key to success is to remain unemotional (no giving in when she starts crying over her gymnastics trophy). "Just say, 'I got tired of looking at it, and you'll find your stuff out in the garage,'" he says.

"My son suddenly wouldn't touch healthy food."
—Samantha Meiler, Millburn, N.J.

The Problem: A 2-year-old whose picky eating went nuclear overnight—he started shunning anything but waffles, grilled cheese, french fries and ice cream. "For six months, we tried reasoning with him," says Meiler.

The Fix: Surprise! "Doing nothing at all," she says. "We put different foods in front of him. If he didn't eat them, we didn't make a big deal about it." (There was always one option they knew he would eat, like fries, in addition to the others.) It wasn't easy. Meiler says she would occasionally leave the room to avoid getting frustrated. But the patience paid off. About a month into the new approach, "he started trying things. Suddenly he was eating chicken, strawberries, raisins, apples, corn. We were diligent about exposing him to new foods, and one day he simply ate them," she says. (Research shows that kids may need to be exposed to a food 15 times before they'll readily eat it.)

The Expert Take: "Hunger becomes a teacher," says Leman. "When a kid refuses to eat something, don't fuss over it." Many parents underestimate the downside of being too pushy, says Long: "Sometimes if we back off, they'll try things on their own. When you're more relaxed, their curiosity can take over."

When Do Babies Stop Being So Darned Cute?

SCIENCE SAYS THAT AFTER 4½, IT'S ALL DOWNHILL ON CUTENESS

BY BONNIE ROCHMAN

A few years ago, my husband chastised me for pandering to Orli, my then-4½-year-old, and youngest, daughter. Half-jokingly, he insinuated that Orli was my favorite.

I've already made clear that it's simply not true. But although I don't prefer one of my kids over the other, it would be hard to argue that Orli's not the cutest. Objectively speaking, of course, they should all win beauty contests, but Orli at that age

geous than adults'. The magic tipping point? Age 4½. That's the age at which "certain crucial infantile facial cues"—the researchers are talking about babies' big eyes and big heads in relation to their smallish noses and mouths—are no longer very noticeable, according to the study, which was published in 2011 in the *Journal of Experimental Child Psychology.*

Wrote Pincott, also the author of *Do Chocolate Lovers Have Sweeter Babies?*: "These cues make us feel soft and protective, whether or not we're biologically relatives—which, in evolutionary terms, increases the likelihood of a baby's survival. (Indeed, studies have found that infants that have tiny eyes, flat foreheads, and square faces, for instance, are less likely to receive attention.)"

I've written before about my trepidation toward becoming a mom of older children. There is something incredibly rewarding about sharing interests and conversations with older kids, about building a relationship based on duality, about watching them learn to play the violin and sew and be named "most improved player" on the basketball team. Yet how I love a cuddly infant.

When Orli was still under 5, with just a few remaining months of preschool left to me, I tried to slow time down, to revel in her joyously nonsensical nature, her proclivity for potty talk, how she irrationally burst into tears when I insisted that she first finish her black beans and cheese before getting a second helping, the way she saucily called me "dude" and then crept into my bed almost every night to hold hands and edge me off my pillow.

She may be past her scientific peak of cuteness, but this mom is still scientifically smitten.

had youth on her side. Her face was still round, her body still squeezable, her baby teeth intact and her syntax to die for. She was little and, therefore, cute. The association transfers to nonhumans as well: puppies elicit more *ooh*s than grown mutts; miniature cupcakes charm more than the larger versions; babies—of any ilk—have more eye appeal.

Perhaps that's why I found a blog post by Jena Pincott on *Psychology Today* so intriguing. It examined this exact phenomenon by way of research that pinpoints at what age babies stop being irresistibly adorable.

Psychologists in China and at the University of Toronto asked adults to gauge the attractiveness of children's faces from infancy to age 6; the study participants found younger kids' faces more likable than those of older children—and way more gor-

Tips for Toddlers

Newborns, unfortunately, do not come with instruction manuals. But that's why we have researchers. In recent years, scientists have been turning up tips on the best ways to raise the littlest children—and some of their advice isn't quite what your mother taught you. **Here are five surprising new tips for better parenting.**

1. Put your baby in a box

It's nothing more than a firm mattress with a sheet on top, tucked inside a cardboard box. But "baby boxes" are catching on as a cheap way to help an infant sleep safely on his back, free of strangulation threats like pillows, toys and blankets. For decades they've been standard issue in Finland, which has one of the world's lowest infant mortality rates. More research is needed to figure out whether the box—or Finland's impressive maternal health care system—deserves the credit. Nonetheless, this year, in an effort to cut down on sudden unexpected infant death, the sleep boxes were made available free by the Baby Box Company to newborns in New Jersey, Alabama and Ohio after parents took a short course about safe sleep practices. Most babies can use them for their first six months.

2. Feed them peanuts

Parents once shielded their babies from the common allergen. But new research shows that exposing children to peanuts early in life lowers their risk of developing an allergy later on. In a landmark move, the National Institute of Allergy and Infectious Diseases issued new guidelines that infants should be introduced to peanut-containing foods starting around six months. Research suggests that doing so may train their immune systems to see the legumes as harmless.

3. Get strict about screens

Raising children in our age of ubiquitous screens isn't easy. Thankfully, in 2016, the American Academy of Pediatrics (AAP) provided some guidance. Kids under 2 years old shouldn't be interacting with screens at all, the AAP says, except to occasionally video chat, and kids ages 2 to 5 should be limited to an hour of quality content each day. New research found that for children under age 2, every additional 30 minutes a day they spent using handheld screens, like smartphones and tablets, meant they were 49% more likely to have speech delays.

4. Tuck your child in by 8

Score one for early bedtimes: preschoolers who go to bed by 8 p.m. are about half as likely to be obese teens as kids who stay up past 9 p.m., according to a recent study in the *Journal of Pediatrics*. Having a regular bedtime seems to deserve part of the credit; another recent study found that 3-year-olds with inconsistent bedtimes were nearly twice as likely to be obese at age 11 as those with regular ones. That may be because children who have a regular early bedtime are more likely to get enough sleep and less likely to stay up late watching TV and snacking, says Sarah Anderson, author of both recent studies and an associate professor of epidemiology at Ohio State University. "Not getting enough sleep can result in changes in the hormones regulating appetite and metabolism," she says.

5. Look out for an unexpected danger

Kids get into everything, and that curiosity can have dire consequences. A 2016 study analyzed emergency department visits at hospitals across the country and found that 1-year-old kids were by far the most likely people to receive treatment for chemical eye burns. That's a surprising discovery, because children, unlike some grown-ups, aren't working with chemicals. Most cases of serious eye injury stemmed from household cleaners that weren't properly stored. An easy solution: lock up chemical cleaners or keep them out of reach.

The Space They Live In

DESIGNING A CHILD'S BEDROOM, FROM BABYHOOD TO TEENHOOD

Newborn to 2 Years

FOCUS ON: The floor

Right now your child is: Using all her senses to take in the world around her (which explains touching the hair of the woman in front of you in the checkout line and tasting the dog's food). It's important for children at this stage to have easy access to their playthings so that they don't just see but also grab, sniff and, yes, chew. "You want your child to have a chance to discover a toy on his own and then examine it in depth to see how it tastes and feels," says Felice Sklamberg, a clinical specialist in pediatric occupational therapy at the New York University Langone Medical Center.

Take advantage by: Grouping like items in soft, low bins (Lego Duplo bricks in one, musical toys in another), recommends Sklamberg: "Babies are easily overstimulated, which makes a catchall toy box overwhelming, not to mention harder to access." Storing items in small bins also makes it easier to swap out toys each week, which is something Sklamberg recommends to avoid sensory overload.

MORE MILESTONES | **4 months**

Weird but true: a child can't taste salt until she hits this mark. (She'll make up for lost time later, when she is introduced to Goldfish.)

5 months

An infant develops a coordinated grasp about now but will still be learning how to disengage physically (read: Let go, already!) until 13 months.

10 months

By now, kids understand the concept of peekaboo. In other words, they realize that Daddy's face doesn't disappear just because he throws a dishcloth over it.

2 years

Go to YouTube and search for "2-Year-Old Genius Nisha," who, at that age, could name around 200 world capitals. (OK, so she was 26 months.)

MORE MILESTONES	**2 years**	**2½ years**	**3 years**
	At 24 months, a child may speak only 50 to 100 words, but she understands most of what you say.	Break out the remote-control cars. It's around now that your little one is capable of pushing simple buttons (not just yours).	This is the age when your child finally begins to stop putting everything in his mouth, because he better distinguishes what is and what is not food.

4 years

And check out this overachiever! Go to https://www.youtube.com/user/falek0 and marvel at now teenage Polish drum prodigy Igor Falecki tap-tap-tapping as a 4-year-old.

2 to 4 Years

FOCUS ON: **A defined play space**

Right now your child is: Starting to focus for longer periods of time. Exactly how long is a matter of temperament. Should your child be particularly single-minded, he may stay occupied for as long as 10 minutes. No need to get out the stopwatch. "Any amount of time, even a minute or two, during which children sit and entertain themselves with one thing helps them grow," says Sklamberg.

Take advantage by: Placing a table and chairs in the child's bedroom to establish a spot for recreation and creativity. In other words, create an ideal place to look at a book or play with a toy. In doing so, notes Sklamberg, "you're introducing kids at an early age to the importance of sitting and focusing." As your child grows and becomes more interested in art, she'll also have a place to sit and spread out. And do yourself a favor: consider investing in kid-size chairs that are comfortable and strong enough for adults too. Though your tot may not want to cuddle up in a glider chair and look at a book during the middle of the day, she may be more engaged by reading a story with you at a table.

4 to 7 Years

FOCUS ON: A comfortable nook

Right now your child is: Into books, whether of the picture-driven, pop-up or prose variety. "Reading is all about using language to open up a world that's not immediately present," says Gillian Dowley McNamee, a professor and the director of teacher education at the Erikson Institute in Chicago. "What matters most for a child in developing this skill is having conversations with a parent about the narrative of a book." Having a welcoming place to read with your child (or children) and to ask questions about the book facilitates this learning process. Books of nursery rhymes or poetry, adds McNamee, can be invaluable in teaching wordplay, a critical step to understanding words in print.

Take advantage by: Creating a cozy reading nook—basically a comfortable chair or a beanbag in close proximity to a bookshelf. As your child becomes increasingly interested in chapter books, which she can read on her own, she may want a reading lamp on her nightstand. (*Anne of Green Gables* can't wait until morning.)

MORE MILESTONES

4 years

Your child now has the motor skills to learn how to play an instrument. Speaking of music, search the internet for Adam Sandler's "Four Years Old," a funny rock ode to this age.

5 years	**6 years**	**7 years**
Children who learn two languages before this point develop a different brain structure than children who learn one.	"What will happen if . . ." is a common thought at this age, which means it's time to break out the science experiments.	In 2000, at the age of 7, Akrit Jaswal of India performed successful hand surgery on his 8-year-old neighbor. How's that for playing doctor?

7 years

Kids become fascinated by something specific and start collections. They also learn about 3,000 new words between now and age 8.

7½ years

Children begin to identify themselves as "athletic" or "unathletic," which can influence their future involvement in sports.

8 years

Farewell, stick people. At this age, children are concerned about depicting the world realistically, and they add an average of 10 parts to a drawing of a person.

10 years

In 1994, at age 10, Michael Kearney became the youngest American college graduate, majoring in anthropology at the University of South Alabama.

7 to 10 Years

FOCUS ON: **The closet**

Right now your child is: "Enjoying satisfaction from completing tasks on her own," says Cora Collette Breuner, an associate professor of pediatrics at the University of Washington. "It's also important to give kids in this age range choices—letting them pick out their own clothes, for example."

Take advantage by: Playing up your child's independence, without creating too much of a headache for yourself. By arranging clothes in an easily navigable way (school clothes on red hangers, weekend wear on yellow ones), you give her a choice ("Pick from the red hangers") with Mom-approved parameters. Additionally, tell her she can have friends over, but only if she makes sure that they clean up after themselves; this is a task she can oversee with the help of accessible storage. "You can ditch the label maker, however," says Pom Shillingford, a New York City–based personal organizer who specializes in families. "Labeling can cause more stress than benefits. It's easier for friends and babysitters to help clean up if there isn't an overly complicated system."

10 to 14 Years

FOCUS ON: The desk

Right now your child is: Capable of handling more responsibility and completing homework assignments on his own—in theory, at least. Reality, however, is another story, says Breuner. "Despite what parenting books may tell you, lower your expectations about how organized the kids, even ones toward the end of this range, can keep their desks and their schoolwork," she says. If you can, place the desk in a spot in the child's bedroom in sight of the door, so you can check in discreetly.

Take advantage by: Establishing a clean work space, with at least four drawers (or compartmentalized shelves), to corral the clutter. "Kids this age are highly distractible. It's easier for a child to spread out books and notes if there's as little as possible to demand his attention," says Breuner. Why four drawers? Donna Goldberg, author of *The Organized Student*, recommends one for basic supplies (pens and pencils), a technology drawer for tablet and camera accessories, one for stationery and paper, and a junk drawer for all the miscellaneous items that can multiply in a child's desk. Another key item: an analog clock kept in plain sight, to boost productivity. "When you look at a digital clock, you're always in the present tense and you don't see time pass," says Goldberg. Finally, it's essential that your child feel involved in the setup process if he's going to have a shot at maintaining the space, says Goldberg.

MORE MILESTONES

10 years

"Um," "like," and "you know" may invade his or her, you know, vocabulary.

13 years

How do they sleep so late? Blame it on biology. The internal clocks of young teens tell them to fall asleep later at night and to snooze longer in the morning.

13½ years

Don't assume teens "should know better." The part of the brain that helps adolescents reason and manage impulses doesn't mature until the 20s.

14 years

At 14, Feliks Zemdegs solved a three-by-three Rubik's cube in eight seconds—and he's gotten better since. To see the Australian teen in action, search YouTube for "Feliks Zemdegs."

CHAPTER TWO

Kids

The Science of Play

RECESS TIME ISN'T JUST
A BREAK FROM SCHOOL.
IT HELPS KIDS LEARN TO
BE HUMAN

BY SIOBHAN O'CONNOR

othing is as natural as a child at play. After a month of little more than eating and sleeping, infants begin to engage in play with their parents and the world around them. Left alone, young children will launch into imaginary play, inventing characters and stories. Put together with peers, children will almost instinctually organize games and activities. Play is so basic to childhood that it is seen even among children in the most dire conditions, in prisons and concentration camps. It is so important to the well-being of children that the United Nations recognizes it as a fundamental human right, on par with the rights to shelter and education. And until recently, American children—finally free from working in the fields or in a factory, as children long had—were allowed to play on their own. In his book *Children at Play: An American History*, writer

Howard Chudacoff describes the first half of the 20th century as a "golden age" of children's playtime.

Yet today, play is something of an endangered activity among American children. A 2011 article from the *American Journal of Play* notes that children's free, unscheduled playtime has been declining steadily over the past half-century. When children do play, it's more likely to be highly structured—think playdates and enrichment classes. Peter Gray, the author of that article and a psychology professor emeritus at Boston College, says the decline in free play is "at least partly because adults have exerted ever-increasing control over children's activities," which should sound familiar to many parents. As even elementary schools come under greater and greater pressure to have their students score well on standardized tests, recess time has been increasingly cut. In 1989, 96% of elementary schools had at least one recess period, yet just a decade later, one survey found that only 70% of even kindergarten classrooms had any recess periods at all.

Gray and other play experts believe these changes have had lasting and negative effects on children. He notes that over the same years that recess and playtime have declined, there have been rises in major depression, anxiety and the suicide rate. "If we love our children and want them to thrive, we must allow them more time and opportunity to play, not less," Gray has written.

Parents and teachers cutting back on children's playtime aren't doing it to be mean—even if it might seem that way to children. They believe that in an increasingly competitive world, there's less time for a kid to be a kid; that is, free, unstructured play doesn't have the payoff that another lesson or test-prep class would. They're restricting playtime because they want their children to thrive. And evolutionary biologists might have once backed them up. Play is, by definition, an activity that has little clear immediate function. That's what separates it from work or education.

But scientists have learned that free play isn't just something children like to do—it's something they need to do. Play keeps kids physically active, all the more important at a

Play is so important to children that the United Nations recognizes it as a fundamental human right.

time when some 20% of American children are obese—more than triple the percentage from the more play-friendly 1970s. (Early activity habits matter—a 2005 study in the *American Journal of Preventive Medicine* found that the most active 9-to-18-year-olds remained the most active later in life.) It also exercises their minds and their creativity. More than anything else, play teaches children how to work together and, at the same time, how to be alone. It teaches them how to be human.

Yet one of the best ways to understand why children play is to look at the behavior of young animals. Primates and many other animals play as juveniles, usually with a characteristic gait or signal that demonstrates to other animals that their activities—which can seem aggressive—aren't meant to be taken seriously, just as children might smile as they play-fight. Play among animals is more conditional on the environment than it appears to be among children—during periods of drought and food scarcity, young animals will cease playing. But play does have a major impact on the brains of animals—and researchers believe it may have a similar impact on the brains of human children.

Rats and cats, like many animals, play with increasing frequency during their juvenile years, before peaking at puberty and, not unlike humans, declining as adults. The development of the cerebellum—the part of the brain that coordinates and regulates muscular activity—follows the same curve, growing rapidly during the juvenile period and then leveling off after puberty. Scientists have theorized that those two facts might be connected. In one experiment, carried out by Sergio Pellis, a neuroscientist at the University of Lethbridge in Alberta, researchers raised two sets of rats from birth, allowing one group to play with other juvenile rats while the other

Why Boys Need to Move in School

SITTING STILL CAN MAKE IT HARD
FOR LITTLE BOYS TO LEARN

BY BELINDA LUSCOMBE

Anybody who has watched little boys for even five seconds knows they are exhausting. At school, they tear around the playground, bolt through corridors and ricochet off classroom walls. According to a recent Finnish study, this is all helping them to be better at reading.

The study, published in the *Journal of Science and Medicine in Sport*, found that the more time boys in first grade spent sitting and the less time they spent being physically active, the fewer gains they made in reading in the two following years. In first grade, a lot of sedentary time and no running around also had a negative impact on their ability to do math.

Among girls, sitting for a long time without moving much didn't seem to have any effect on their ability to learn.

Researchers at the University of Eastern Finland analyzed studies that measured physical activity and sedentary time of 153 kids ages 6 to 8. The studies used a combined heart-rate and movement sensor, and researchers gave kids standardized tests in math and reading. "We found that lower levels of moderate to vigorous physical activity, higher levels of sedentary time, and particularly their combination, were related to poorer reading skills in boys," the study says.

While the test group was small and Scandinavian (the Finnish school system's freaky success is almost legendary), the study offers some evidence for what parents have been thinking for a long time: we may not be educating boys the right way.

As pressure increases on schools to show evidence of learning, many education systems have tried to provide a more academically rich environment. But sometimes this has come at the cost of physical education, which is often considered an optional extra rather than one of the core skills a student must master.

Money and school hours that might have been spent on P.E. are now devoted to additional classroom time and technology. Computers, laptops and tablets are worthy teaching tools, but they promote a very sedentary style of learning. Add to this the reliance on testing, which, again, has its merits, and you have kids sitting down for longer and longer periods every day. Most U.S. schools don't require any P.E. or recess.

The connection between exercise and learning is not new, but the Finnish study provides stronger objective evidence that the increased emphasis on sedentary academic activity among the youngest learners may be fruitless if it comes at the cost of physical activity. Boys whose days were more sedentary when they were in first grade (a crucial year for learning to read) not only made fewer gains in reading in second and third grade but also did worse at math for that year. The authors aren't sure why the difference between boys and girls is so stark. Not as many girls participated in the study, so that may have influenced results. Also, although it is likely that physical activity has the same effect on the brains of boys and girls, for girls, academic achievement may be more influenced by factors such as parental educational support, peer acceptance, teachers' positive attitudes and their own motivation.

group was kept from playing but otherwise had normal interactions with adult rats. At puberty, the rats were euthanized and dissected. Rats raised in the environment without play showed a more immature pattern of neurons in the prefrontal cortex—the center of the brain in mammals—than did rats who had been allowed to play.

Pellis believes that playing while young helps an animal—and potentially a child—selectively prune the overabundance of cortical brain cells that exist at birth, aiding in the process of maturation. The brain rewires itself under the positive stress of play, as children figure out how to navigate the world and each other.

The apparent randomness of play may be its secret genius. Part of what sets humans apart from other animals is the range of creativity,

Free play encourages the development of the two skills that no robot can replace: creativity and teamwork.

flexibility and adaptation. That's precisely what free play—play without the encircling structure of adults—helps promote. Children who can entertain themselves, or play with one another, are unconsciously learning how to adapt themselves to challenges they'll face further down the road. This is especially true of the pretend play that is most characteristic of human children. (Rats, as far as we know, do not have imaginary friends.) Play, in this way, can be thought of as education by another name—which is another reason we should be concerned that free playtime is now being taken up by structured activities or screen time.

Play also has a vital social drive, as education experts Olivia Saracho and Bernard Spodek have described. Anyone who has observed a school playground knows that children can instantly organize themselves to play in groups. Playing together—and playing with parents—helps children learn to predict and respond to another's shifting movements

and to interpret their desires. It helps them learn how to work together in groups and to share, negotiate and resolve conflicts—especially if parents and other adults give children the space they need to work out problems on their own. Working with juvenile rats, neuroscientist Jaak Panksepp of Washington State University found that play actually changes the brain to make it more pro-social. Of the 1,200 neocortical genes that Panksepp looked at in one rat experiment, about one third of them showed significant changes in activity after just a half-hour of play.

The good news is that after years of cutting back on free playtime for children, smart schools and parents are beginning to understand the benefits of letting kids of all ages roam relatively free. In 2013 the American Academy of Pediatrics' Council on School Health released a statement arguing that "safe and well-supervised recess offers cognitive, social, emotional, and physical benefits that may not be fully appreciated when a decision is made to diminish it." At Texas Christian University, Debbie Rhea developed what she calls the LiiNK program, which stands for "Let's inspire innovation 'n kids." Children in kindergarten and first grade in the program, which has been tried out in a handful of schools in Texas, are sent out to recess as often as four times a day, in short bursts that add up to an hour. That ensures that the youngest children get more than enough free playtime while encouraging them to sit still when they are in the classroom, knowing a break isn't too far away.

In an age of standardized testing and intense academic competition, it's easy to believe that play is one more thing American children will have to do without. But free play encourages the development of the two skills that no robot can replace: creativity and teamwork. Just as the most imaginative and innovative leaders in business and politics needed time away from work to come up with some of their best ideas, so do children need time to play on their own, away from schools and screens and even adults. The payoff will be there down the line—and even more than that, it will be felt here and now. Because let's not forget—play is fun. That's the whole point.

Secrets of Birth Order

FIRSTBORN OR LAST, WHERE YOU FALL IN YOUR FAMILY CAN HAVE SURPRISING INFLUENCE THROUGHOUT YOUR LIFE

BY JEFFREY KLUGER

It could not have been easy being Elliott Bulloch Roosevelt. If the alcohol wasn't getting him, the morphine was. If it wasn't the morphine, it was the struggle with depression. Then, of course, there were the constant comparisons with big brother Teddy.

In 1883, the year Elliott began battling melancholy, Teddy had already published his first book and been elected to the New York State Assembly. By 1891—about the time Elliott, still unable to establish a career, had to be institutionalized to deal with his addictions—Teddy was U.S. civil service commissioner and the author of eight books. Three years later, Elliott, 34, died just days after what was believed to have been a suicide attempt. Seven years after that, Teddy, 42, became president.

It can't be easy being a runt in a litter that includes a president. But it couldn't have been easy, either, being Billy Ripken, an unexceptional major league infielder craning his neck for notice while the press swarmed around Hall of Famer and elder brother Cal. It couldn't have been easy being Eli Manning, who entered the NFL as a raw rookie in 2004 even as his older brother Peyton was already being talked about as a future Hall of Famer for the Indianapolis Colts.

Of all the things that shape who we are, few seem more arbitrary than the sequence in which we and our siblings pop out of the womb. But in family after family, case study after case study, the simple roll of the birth-date dice has an odd and arbitrary power all its own. Firstborns, a group of Norwegian investigators has found, enjoy a three-point IQ advantage over the next eldest—probably a result of the intellectual boost that comes from mentoring their younger siblings and helping them in day-to-day tasks.

Studies in the Philippines show that later-born siblings tend to be shorter and weigh less than earlier-borns. Other studies show that younger siblings are less likely to be vaccinated than older ones, with last-borns getting immunized sometimes at only half the rate of firstborns. Eldest siblings are also disproportionately represented in high-paying professions. Younger siblings, by contrast, are looser cannons, less educated and less strapping, perhaps, but statistically likelier to live the exhilarating life of an artist or a comedian, an adventurer or a firefighter. And middle children? Well, they can be a puzzle—even to researchers.

"There are stereotypes out there about birth order, and very often those stereotypes are spot-on," says Delroy Paulhus, a professor of psychology at the University of British Columbia in Vancouver. "I think this is one of those cases in which people just figured things out on their own."

Humans aren't alone in the birth-order game. All manner of species devote more resources to older chicks, calves and cubs than to younger ones, protecting their existing genetic investment before expending limited assets on a newer model.

We don't like to see our species as coming from the same coldly pragmatic traditions, but we face many of the same pressures. As recently as 100 years ago, children in many areas of the U.S. had only about a 50% chance of surviving into adulthood, and in less developed parts of the world, the odds remain daunting. It can be a sensible strategy to have multiple offspring to continue your line in case some are claimed by disease or injury, but that means food, attention and money can get stretched thinner and thinner, and it's later-borns—even in developed countries—who pay the price.

Catherine Salmon, a professor of psychol-

ogy at the University of Redlands in California, laments that it can often be hard to collect enough subjects for birth-order studies from the average student body, since the campus population is typically overweighted with eldest sibs. "Families invest a lot in the firstborn," she says.

All of this favoritism can become self-reinforcing. As parental pampering produces a fitter, smarter, more confident firstborn, Mom and Dad are likely to invest even more in that child, placing their bets on an offspring who is likelier to thrive—and thrive they do. In a survey of corporate heads conducted by Vistage, an international organization of CEOs, poll takers reported that 43% of the people who occupy the big chair in boardrooms are firstborns, 33% are middle-borns and 23% are last-borns. Eldest siblings are disproportionately represented among surgeons, MBAs and the U.S. Congress too.

For those firstborns, this is a pretty sweet deal, but younger siblings see things different-

dimension of temperament known as conscientiousness—a sense of general responsibility and follow-through—later-borns score higher on what's known as agreeableness, or the simple ability to get along in the world.

"Kids recognize a good low-power strategy," says Frank Sulloway, a psychologist at the University of California, Berkeley, who has spent decades studying birth order.

Later-borns are also willing to take risks with their physical safety. All sibs are equally likely to be involved in sports, but younger ones are likelier to choose the kinds that could cause injury. "They don't go out for tennis," Sulloway says. "They go out for rugby, ice hockey." Even when siblings play the same sport, they play it differently. Sulloway once conducted a study of brothers who were major league ballplayers and found that the elder brothers excel at skills that involve less physical danger—playing the outfield, say. Younger siblings are the ones who put themselves in harm's way—crouching down in catcher's gear to block an incoming runner or risking a collision with an infielder while trying to steal a base.

Ben Dattner, a business consultant who also teaches industrial and organizational psychology at New York University, has found that even when later-borns take conservative jobs in the corporate world, they approach their work in a high-wire way. Firstborn CEOs do best when they're making incremental improvements in their companies: shedding underperforming products, maximizing profits from existing lines and generally making sure the trains run on time. Later-born CEOs are more inclined to blow up the trains and lay new track. "Later-borns are better at transformational change," says Dattner. "They pursue riskier, more innovative, more creative approaches."

If eldest sibs are the dogged achievers and youngest sibs are the gamblers and visionaries, where does this leave those in between? That it's so hard to define what middle-borns become is largely due to the fact that it's so hard to define who they are growing up. The youngest in the family, but only until someone else comes along, they are both teacher and student, babysitter and babysat, too

ly and struggle early on to shake up the existing order. They clearly don't have size on their side, as their physically larger siblings keep them in line with what researchers euphemistically call a "high-power strategy" and what the rest of us might recognize as bullying. But there are low-power strategies too, and one of the most effective ones is humor. It's awfully hard to resist the charms of someone who can make you laugh, and families abound with stories of last-borns who are the clowns of the brood, able to get their way simply by being funny or outrageous. Birth-order scholars often observe that some of history's great satirists—Voltaire, Mark Twain—were among the youngest members of large families, a pattern that continues today. Late-night host Stephen Colbert—who yields to no one in his ability to get a laugh—often points out that he's the last of 11 children.

Such examples might be little more than anecdotal, but personality tests show that although firstborns score especially well on the young for the privileges of the firstborn but too old for the latitude given the last.

Stuck for life in a center seat, middle children get shortchanged even on family resources. Unlike firstborns, who spend at least some time in the beginning of their lives as only-child eldests, and last-borns, who hang around long enough to become only-child youngests, middlings are never alone and thus never get 100% of the parents' investment of time and money.

"There is a U-shaped distribution in which the oldest and youngest get the most," says Sulloway. That may take an emotional toll. Sulloway cites other studies in which the self-esteem of first-, middle- and last-borns is plotted on a graph and follows the same curvilinear trajectory.

The phenomenon known as de-identification may also work against a middle-born. Siblings who hope to stand out in a family often do so by observing what the elder child does—and then doing the opposite. If the firstborn gets good grades and takes an after-school job, the second-born may go the slacker route. The third-born may then de-de-identify, opting for industriousness, even if in the more unconventional ways of the last-born.

But there are welcome compensations to being the middle-born, not the least being their tendency to develop deeper and broader social circles than their siblings. Perhaps this is a result of their emotional needs not being met as fully at home, but they spin this disadvantage into a powerful advantage, forging the kind of community of friends and colleagues that can pay enormous dividends outside the home.

Ultimately, of course, birth order will never be a precise science. Individual families are just too sloppy for that—a mishmash of competing needs and moods and emotions, better understood by the people in the thick of them than by any investigator standing outside. Yet millennia of families would swear by the power of birth order to shape the adults we eventually become. We may leave the nest comparatively early in life, but the influence of the chicks with whom we shared it stays with us forever.

Music Can Alter Your Child's Brain

EVEN KIDS WHO HATE THE BAND WILL BENEFIT FROM LEARNING MUSIC

BY MELISSA LOCKER

There's little doubt that learning to play a musical instrument is great for developing brains. Science has shown that when children learn to play music, their brains begin to hear and process sounds that they couldn't otherwise hear. This helps them develop "neurophysiological distinction" between certain sounds that can aid in literacy, which can translate into improved academic results for kids.

Many parents read the above sentence and started mentally googling child music classes in their local area. But if your kid doesn't like learning an instrument or doesn't actively engage in the class—opting to stare at the wall or doodle in a notebook instead of participating—he or she may not be getting all the benefits of those classes anyway.

A 2014 study from Northwestern University revealed that in order to fully reap the cognitive benefits of a music class, kids can't just sit there and let the sound of music wash over them. They have to be actively engaged in the music and participate in the class. "Even in a group of highly motivated students, small variations in music engagement—attendance and class participation—predicted the strength of neural processing after music training," according to Nina Kraus, the director of Northwestern's Auditory Neuroscience Laboratory. She coauthored the study with Jane Hornickel, Dana L. Strait, Jessica Slater and Elaine Thompson of Northwestern University.

Additionally, the study showed that students who played instruments in class had more improved neural encoding of speech than children who attended a music appreciation group. "We like to say that 'making music matters,' " said Kraus. "Because it is only through the active generation and manipulation of sound that music can rewire the brain."

Kraus, whose research appeared in *Frontiers in Psychology*, continued: "Our results support the importance of active experience and meaningful engagement with sound to stimulate changes in the brain." Active participation and meaningful engagement translate into children being highly involved in their musical training—these are the kids who had good attendance, who paid close attention in class "and were the most on-task during their lesson," said Kraus.

To find these results, Kraus's team went straight to the source, using sensitive Intelligent Hearing Systems technology to capture the students' brains' responses.

Kraus's team at Northwestern teamed up with the Harmony Project, a music program serving low-income children in Los Angeles, after Harmony's founder, Margaret Martin, approached Kraus to provide evidence behind the program's success with students.

According to the Harmony Project's website, since 2008, 93% of Harmony Project seniors have gone on to college, despite a dropout rate of 50% or higher in their neighborhoods. It's a pretty impressive achievement, and the Northwestern team designed a study to explore those striking numbers. That research, published in the *Journal of Neuroscience*, offered persuasive evidence that music training has a biological effect on children's developing nervous systems.

As a follow-up, the team decided to test whether the level of engagement in that music training actually matters. Turns out, it really does. Researchers found that after two years, children who not only regularly attended music classes but also actively participated in

There's little doubt that learning to play a musical instrument is great for developing brains.

the classes showed larger improvements in how the brain processes speech and reading scores than their less-involved peers.

"It turns out that playing a musical instrument is important," Kraus said, differentiating her group's findings from the now-debunked myth that just listening to certain types of music improves intelligence—the so-called Mozart effect. "We don't see these kinds of biological changes in people who are just listening to music, who are not playing an instrument," said Kraus. "I like to give the analogy that you're not going to become physically fit just by watching sports." It's important to engage with the sound in order to reap the benefits and see changes in the central nervous system.

As to how to keep children interested in playing instruments, that's up to the parents. "I think parents should follow their intuitions with respect to keeping their children engaged," said Kraus. "Find the kind of music they love, good teachers, an instrument they'll like. Making music should be something that children enjoy and will want to keep doing for many years!"

With that in mind, it's not too late to encourage the kids in your life to set aside the Minecraft Legos, Xbox games and GoldieBlox and help them instead discover the joys—and reap the benefits—of music lessons.

How to Raise Hopeful Kids

OPTIMISM—IN THE RIGHT DOSES—
CAN HELP MAKE CHILDREN
RESILIENT IN THE FACE OF LIFE'S
SETBACKS

BY DAVID BJERKLIE

I t's the Force, just like in *Star Wars*," says Ethan Tassiuk excitedly. "It is the strongest feeling, deep, deep, deep down inside of your heart, a feeling that no matter how hard it gets and how much it hurts, that there is another way to go on." Yes, says Ethan with a nod, this is what *niraijungniq* (the Inuktitut word for "hope") means to him.

It is a late June evening, still bathed in twilight, in the Inuit community of Arviat, on Hudson Bay, in the Canadian Arctic territory of Nunavut. Ethan sits at a dining-room table fielding questions about the power of hope. The questions are being asked by a friend, Arviat TV co-producer Jamie Bell. Bell has known the 19-year-old since Ethan was a shy 12-year-old showing up for his first meeting of the Arviat Film Society, a group of young community filmmakers who have made films on topics such as suicide prevention and bullying, relationships, sexual health, the wisdom of elders—and even an Arctic horror movie.

It is an especially poignant conversation because hope—or its absence—is at the heart of nearly everything in Arviat,

Top: An Inuit child plays in Arviat, Nunavut; bottom: the Canadian town of Arviat is home to nearly 3,000 people.

a community rich in Inuit culture and traditions but one that also struggles with isolation, poverty, unemployment and suicide. How do you measure hope? How do you support it and share it? For the people of Arviat—for all of us—how do you impart hope to the next generation?

Hope is fundamental to humanity, but that doesn't mean we don't have very mixed views about it. In Greek mythology, Zeus cursed humankind for the actions of Prometheus, who stole fire from the gods, by giving Pandora a vessel she was not to open under any circumstances. When she disobeyed, out streamed all the evils of the world. Only hope remained, by which the torments of mortality might be endured.

Yet several Greek philosophers saw hope as only one more torment. Sophocles considered it a human foible that only prolonged suffering. Euripides saw it as a "curse upon humanity." Twenty-three hundred years later, 19th-century German philosophers Arthur Schopenhauer and Friedrich Nietzsche also rejected hope as folly and false promise; Nietzsche, in fact, thought that of all the torments Zeus had brought down on humans, hope was the worst.

But hope has its champions, too. Psychologists understand hope as what links our goals with the means by which we pursue them. Yes, hope can be empty or desperate, but it also embodies our desires, our determination and our expectations of success. Think in terms of the children's classic *The Little Engine That Could*, whose titular subject's goal of delivering toys, dolls, fresh fruit and milk to the kids who lived over the mountain began with "I think I can, I think I can" and ended with "I thought I could, I thought I could."

The most prominent modern theorist of hope, the psychologist C.R. Snyder, also thought of hope as a journey. In addition to a destination, the journey requires a map and means of transportation (what Snyder referred to as waypower) and the energy and determination (the willpower) to put the plan into motion.

The foundations of hope, according to Snyder and his colleagues, begin early in life. Newborns quickly learn the connection of

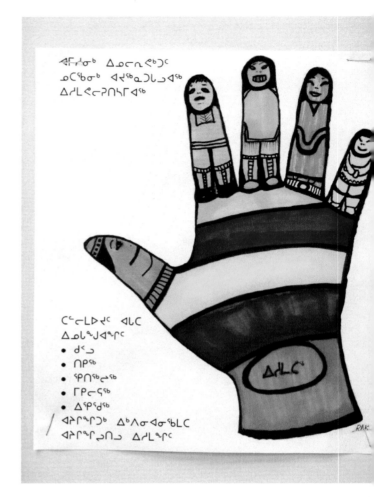

goals and agency "because their survival depends on such 'this follows that' chronologies," he wrote. Infants refine their abilities as "they anticipate and plan for events," which leads to learning to point to desired objects, which in turn "signals the infant's ability to single out one goal and even recruit an adult's help to obtain it."

Believing that goals are achievable is what many kids find difficult. Kids with pessimistic explanatory styles often see their problems as originating from within and likely to be open-ended and permanent, while optimists see adversity as coming from external sources and likely to be specific and temporary. In this sense, hope is a theory of a child's world. "I wouldn't think of it as innate, however," says David Anderson, senior director of ADHD and Behavior Disorders at the Child Mind Institute in New York. "Kids are influenced by so many

Left: The power of family and Inuit community and culture are used in the schools in art and education programs. Above: In a community where nearly 40% of the population is under age 14, hope is both a challenge and an opportunity.

factors. We all fall into behavioral patterns, ways we automatically think about things."

These patterns can become part of our personal narratives, the stories we tell ourselves about who we are and how we got here, as well as where we've been, where we're headed and how far we can go. Such patterns of thought can become ingrained, but fortunately they may not be quite as hard to undo as we might assume. "What we are trying to do when kids come in with symptoms of depression or anxiety is to identify the patterns of thinking that lead to their feelings of hopelessness," says Anderson. "We help them talk back to their thoughts, to initiate patterns that are more likely to lead to a sense of hope. We help them think about problems as solvable, as challenges they can face and break down into smaller pieces. All of these tools are in the service of building hope for the future, a sense

that things can change and get better."

Goals can range from specific and immediate to abstract and remote. "One of the keys to helping kids is looking at their goals," says Beth Doll, a professor of educational psychology at the University of Nebraska. "What do they want to achieve? What do they want to accomplish? For younger kids, those are going to be goals over a few weeks or a few months. With older kids, we're looking at goals over a year. And by the time they are juniors and seniors, we start to see goals over a lifetime."

As is the case for the closely related research subjects of optimism, resilience and grit, there is no consensus on how malleable our sense of hope is. Certainly a great many factors, from neurological to familial to social, interact to bolster children's sense of hope—or rob them of it. While researchers try to untangle the interactions, mental-health professionals, as well as educators, meet hope where it lives. The goal is to encourage and cultivate the sense of hope in all children but never blame the hopeless. "There's no specifically hope-focused intervention," says Anderson. "We don't diagnose anything based on hope. But much of what we do, in cognitive behavior therapy and other treatment, centers on building hope."

A key component of these efforts is the social-emotional-learning programs many schools are adopting. "I think there's increasing recognition of how social, emotional and cognitive functioning are intermingled," says researcher Lisa Flook of the University of Wisconsin. "The potential impact of such programs in the forefront of education is enormous." Anderson believes this is already happening: "One of the most encouraging trends we are seeing is that schools are recognizing how closely connected mental health and academic performance are."

A generation ago, Snyder and his colleagues believed that "hopeful thinking can empower and guide a lifetime of learning." As Jamie and Ethan know from their experiences working with the youth in Arviat, it can also empower lives. "What gives people the strength to have hope?" That's a great question, says Bell. "Because when we ask how it works, the answers help us build hope in ways we can share."

Autism and Genius

RESEARCHERS ARE FINDING A LINK BETWEEN AUTISM AND CHILDREN WHO BECOME PRODIGIES

BY JOANNE RUTHSATZ AND KIMBERLY STEPHENS

rwin Nyiregyházi's keen ear for music was obvious almost immediately. The Budapest-born musician tried to imitate singing before his first birthday. At 3 (and before he had ever taken a lesson), he began improvising and composing on the piano. He gave frequent recitals in the homes of wealthy Hungarians, and, at 8, he performed for the British royal family in London.

In 1910, Géza Révész, a lecturer at the University of Budapest, began studying a then 7-year-old Erwin. Révész ultimately published a book, *The Psychology of a Musical Prodigy*, in which he documented Erwin's development over several years. The last composition Erwin sent to Révész was from the spring of 1914, when Erwin was 11. Of his subsequent development, Révész reported, "I regret to say I know nothing."

A child prodigy is defined in the scholarly literature as someone who performs at an adult professional level in a demanding field before adolescence. The question of what becomes of such children when they grow up is intriguing. The media occasionally reported about Erwin, and a biographer later wrote an account of his life. But from a scientific perspective, there was nothing. Some might say he "fell off a cliff."

That phrase—"falling off a cliff"—is often used in the context of autism to describe the transition from adolescence to adulthood. According to a study published in 2011, many autistic young adults experience a "steep drop" in services after high school. The availability of relevant research similarly plummets.

As we recount in our book *The Prodigy's Cousin*, there are many hidden links between autism and prodigy. Child prodigies aren't typically autistic, but they have extreme working memories, excellent attention to detail and a striking passion for their area of interest (imagine a kid who paints every day after kindergarten, devours images of Georgia O'Keeffe's art and begins showing her own work at 7). These traits are also associated with autism. Many child prodigies have autistic family members, and there's even preliminary evidence that prodigy and autism may share a genetic link.

Unfortunately, a lack of research into the full life span is one more thing that the two have in common. No one really knows what becomes of child prodigies as adults. While there have been longitudinal studies of children with extremely high IQs, nothing similar exists for truly prodigious children.

There's a similar drop-off in autism research when it comes to adulthood. As Nancy Minshew, the director of the Center for Excellence in Autism Research at the University of

Erwin Nyiregyházi with the
film star Gloria Swanson
before a 1937 concert

Parents and Autism

CAREGIVERS CAN HELP REDUCE THE EFFECTS OF AUTISM IN CHILDREN

BY ALEXANDRA SIFFERLIN

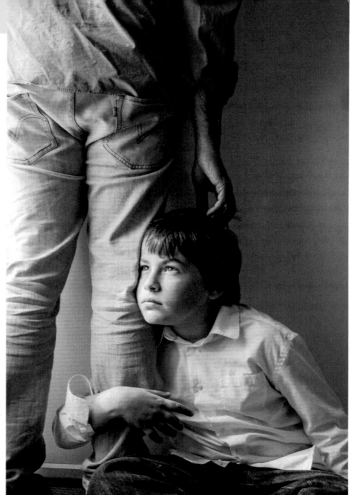

Although there's no cure for autism, studies suggest that interventions can help improve some of the common developmental issues that accompany the disorder. A 2016 study showed that one intervention in particular, led by the parents of children with autism, can reduce some symptoms of the disease over several years.

In the report, published in the journal *The Lancet*, U.K. researchers looked at the results of a study called the Preschool Autism Communication Trial. In that study, 152 kids from ages 2 to 4 were randomly assigned to a year of a parent-led intervention, in which their parents interacted with them and received feedback from a therapist, in addition to treatment as usual. The other group received normal treatment as usual without the parental intervention.

In the parenting group, the parents were filmed, and later they watched the videos with a therapist to discuss the interactions. For example, a child might make a vocalization that may not be very clear or even seem directed at the parent but is a try at communicating, says study author Tony Charman, chair in clinical child psychology at King's College London. "Sometimes it might be natural for a parent at the beginning of the therapy to not notice that attempt at communication," he says. "The therapist can help the parent see

that as an opportunity: how can they respond or locate those cues?"

The parents had 12 therapy sessions over six months and then received support each month for another six months. Six years later, the researchers analyzed 121 of the original children from the study and assessed their autism severity based on a standard measurement scale that looks at the child's symptoms. The children started the study with similar scores, but after six years, the kids who had the intervention early in life scored better. Those children had 17% fewer symptoms than their peers; they had better communication skills and were less likely to show repetitive behaviors. The children did not appear to have notable improvements in their language skills or anxiety levels from the therapy, however.

"We think the results are encouraging and even possibly

somewhat surprising," says Charman. "This follow-up took place six years after a one-year treatment had ended, and an awful lot of things would've happened to these children in the meantime."

Charman says the fact that the children showed increases in their communication skills over the long term "is remarkable and isn't something people have been able to demonstrate up until this point." There are also benefits for parents who use this form of therapy, who are sometimes confused, bewildered and distressed by the behavior of their young children, he says. "You are changing the understanding the parent has of their young child," says Charman. "This intervention is giving them tools to improve their interactions and see the communication developing with their children, and that's quite empowering for parents."

Pittsburgh, said, though autistic adults have been involved in neuroscience and genetics studies, the research landscape "has been a desert" when it comes to adult treatments and other adulthood-specific issues. The scientists Patricia Howlin and Julie Lounds Taylor characterized autism in adulthood as "woefully under-researched" in a 2015 special issue of the journal *Autism*. In 2011, another team wrote that research on older adults with autism was "practically nonexistent."

One obstacle to studying autism in adulthood has been finding autistic adult participants. Lisa Gilotty, the chief of the autism research program at the National Institute of Mental Health, said that those reviewing study proposals were once skeptical of the feasibility of large-scale autism-in-adulthood studies. Autistic children could be located through schools and early-intervention programs, but it was difficult to put together a sizable cohort of autistic adults. But in recent years, Gilotty said, she has seen more researchers assemble adult subjects and begin building larger cohorts of participants.

> ## Childhood is an important time for the autistic, the prodigious and for more typically developing kids, but it's only the beginning of the story.

It can also be difficult to find a group of prodigies to follow into adulthood. One of us, Joanne Ruthsatz, has assembled a cohort of more than 30 of these children, which makes for the largest-ever prodigy research sample. Almost all of these prodigies are still young, and their trajectories largely remain to be seen. But the oldest among them are mostly still pursuing the specialties that made them prodigies in the first place. There's no reason to think that there's anything to the idea of "early ripe, early rot" for prodigies. But if it turned out that these kids were especially vulnerable at particular points in their lives, wouldn't that be something worth knowing?

Just as seems to be the case with prodigy, autism in adulthood varies a great deal by person. But some of the early studies on autistic adults present a troubling picture. The authors of a 2012 study found that more than half of the autistic individuals who had left high school in the previous two years had not held a paid job or gone to school, a higher percentage than those with a learning disability, an intellectual disability or a speech/language impairment.

Autistic adults also report more difficulty communicating with their health-care providers and more unmet medical needs than non-autistic adults. They have increased rates of medical conditions ranging from depression to diabetes to Parkinson's disease. Mortality rates are higher for those with autism.

In recent years, scientists have piloted promising new interventions and supports for autistic adults. For example, a team of researchers at the University of Pittsburgh (including Minshew) investigating the feasibility and efficacy of cognitive-enhancement therapy for autistic adults achieved promising results in a small, 18-month study. Other research suggests that virtual-reality training for job interviews may improve self-confidence and performance for autistic adults. A team that investigated Project SEARCH, a supported internship model, found that autistic students who participated in the program seemed to have a greater likelihood of finding paid work after high school.

But there is still much more to be done to address questions about autism in adulthood, which include: What most improves quality of life for the autistic? How can we increase autism awareness and acceptance? And which autism interventions are effective for adults?

Childhood is an important time for the autistic, the prodigious and for more typically developing kids, but it's only the beginning of the story.

Tips for Kids

Raising a child in the 21st century isn't easy. You have more information at your fingertips than ever before, but that deluge can leave you conflicted and confused.

Here, then, are five basic things to keep in mind.

1. Encourage them not to sit still

What's true for you is true for them, too: exercise is good for the body and the mind. Research shows that kids who move more have longer attention spans, get higher grades and do better on standardized tests than less-active children. New research is adding to those benefits. A study of first-graders found that boys who moved around more and sat less tended to have better reading and math skills than those who were less active, and one 2017 study of 800 6-year-olds found that children who exercised more had fewer symptoms of depression years later on.

2. Try mindfulness

Research is mounting that mindfulness helps kids of all ages, from preschool to high school. Elementary-school-age kids may especially stand to benefit: recent research has found that first-, second- and third-graders who were taught mindfulness and breathing techniques had fewer symptoms of ADHD and less test anxiety. Even for kids without these issues, mindfulness has been shown to increase kindness, sleep quality, behavioral control, concentration and even math scores.

3. Teach your kids empathy

"Young children are egocentric by nature," says Michele Borba, a psychologist and the author of the recent parenting book *UnSelfie: Why Empathetic Kids Succeed in Our All-About-Me World.* "But we parents must help them think 'we,' not 'me'—especially if they are to survive and thrive in today's plugged-in, accelerated, me-first world." Borba interviewed 500 altruistic kids for her book and found that a common trait among them was having parents who both modeled kindness and expected the same of their kids. "The easiest way to tune up kindness is tune it up in ourselves, so our children catch our example," Borba says. There are lots of little opportunities to teach empathy, and it starts with being able to recognize the emotions of others. Even pets can help with that, Borba says: watch the puppy's tail, and you'll know when she's happy.

4. Emphasize effort over ability

Girls tend to do better in school than boys. Even so, many fall prey to the "boys are smarter" stereotype that affects how they see their gender from an alarmingly young age. A recent study published in the journal *Science* found that starting at age 6, girls were much less likely to believe that members of their sex were "really, really smart" and instead believed that boys belonged more to that category. (In contrast, 5-year-old girls readily classified their own gender as smart.) It's not hard to see how this affects girls' lives later on; women are much less likely to go into careers like science and engineering. Emphasize the value of learning and effort, instead of natural talent, with praise like "I like that you worked hard on this and found a great way to do it," says study author Andrei Cim-pian, an associate professor of psychology at New York University. "When given praise such as this, children are more resilient to failure because they understand what to do differently the next time around; 'you're smart' doesn't tell you what to do when you're having difficulties."

5. Validate their worries

Anxiety is on the rise in children today. About 30% of girls and 20% of boys have had an anxiety disorder, according to the National Institute of Mental Health. To comfort an anxious child, a parent instinctively might tell them everything will be OK, says Jill Emanuele, the senior director of the Mood Disorders Center at the Child Mind Institute. But the anxiety will inevitably return—sometimes even more strongly.

Instead, offer your support by acknowledging anxiety for what it is, which may help kids realize they can control it. Try phrases such as "It looks like those worry thoughts are back again" or "What you just said sounds like your anxiety is trying to bully you again," Emanuele recommends.

"In therapy, children are taught skills for managing anxiety, such as deep breathing, which allow them to take charge of the situation and fight the anxiety rather than avoid it," Emanuele says. Supportive tools like these can empower kids to confront their own fears.

Being 12

TEXT AND PHOTOGRAPHS BY
JULIANA SOHN

T he age of 12 is a cusp year, a year of tremendous change both emotionally and physically. Although everyone matures at different rates, 12 is the age when many girls in middle school start their period and begin to exert their independence. It is a beautiful, tumultuous, exhilarating and often confusing time.

As a photographer, I've had the chance to document this period of transition with several 12-year-olds in New York City and talk with them about their lives. It's an opportunity for these girls to have a voice and make a visual statement about who they are at this vital moment.

Simone

"Being 12 is like being on a never-ending roller coaster. It was hard, with a lot of scary and new experiences. I found comfort in old habits from childhood that made me feel safe and happy. My singing was my confidence and guided me through a difficult year of change."

Sachary
"I'm me in my city."

Lola
"When I got my head shaved, I felt confident. It meant I was no longer a random kid in my class. Every time someone complimented my new hair, it felt like people finally were learning to accept what I liked and who I was. It felt amazing."

Chloe

"When you grow up, your life becomes so much more difficult; you start to see everything isn't as easy as it once was. The changes in my body and emotions are sometimes scary."

Ariel

"I have always been an early riser. I wake long before the sun rises every day. Waking up early gives me time to contemplate, draw and finish up my schoolwork. I enjoy sitting on the windowsill and watching the sun rise."

Isadora

"When I went to the March on Washington, I felt like I was a part of current events. I felt like I was doing something powerful and standing for what I believe in. I think it's important to voice my opinion and be a part of her-story."

Megan
"You never feel 12 until you're 13."

Betty
"Twelve was the year I really started taking charge of my own life and responsibility for my actions. I don't really know why . . . maybe it was transitioning to eighth grade, or my bat mitzvah, but 12 made me a stronger and more powerful person."

CHAPTER THREE

Teens

Inside the Teen Brain

IT'S NOT YOU. RESEARCHERS ARE
FINDING THAT TEENAGE BRAINS
REALLY ARE SPECIAL

BY ALEXANDRA SIFFERLIN

hen Frances Jensen's eldest son, Andrew, reached high school, he underwent a transformation. Frances's calm, predictable child changed his hair color from brown to black and started wearing bolder clothing. It felt as if he turned into an angst-filled teenager overnight. Jensen, now the chair of the neurology department at the Perelman School of Medicine at the University of Pennsylvania, wondered what happened and whether Andrew's younger brother would undergo the same metamorphosis. So she decided to use her skills as a neuroscientist to explore what was happening under the hood. "I realized I had an experiment going on in my own home," says Jensen, author of *The Teenage Brain*.

That was around 10 years ago, when society at large was only beginning to catch up to the idea that the teen brain was not a fully developed adult brain, just with less mileage. For generations, the overarching thinking was that the brain had reached its full growth by the time a child reached puberty. But thanks to the research of people like Jensen and many others, beginning in the 1990s, it's become clear that the teenage brain is some-

thing much more complex—and special.

Doctors, parents and teachers have long held preconceived notions about why teenagers act so reckless and emotional, and many of these explanations have turned out to be incorrect. It was once believed that teens were impulsive due to raging hormones and that they were difficult because they hated authority. But advances in brain imaging, which gathered force in the 2000s, told a much more complicated story. It turns out the teenage brain is nowhere near fully baked and that the brain's structure and its effects on development continue into a person's 20s.

Advanced brain imaging has revealed that the teenage brain has lots of plasticity, which means it can change, adapt and respond to its environment. The brain does not grow by getting substantially larger during the teenage years but rather through increased connectivity between brain regions. This growth in connectivity presents itself as white matter in the brain, which comes from a fatty substance called myelin. As the brain develops, myelin wraps itself around nerve cells' axons—long, thin tendrils that extend from the cell and transmit information—like insulation on an electrical wire. Myelination, the scientific name for this process, strengthens and accelerates the communication between brain regions and underlies a person's basic learning abilities.

The myelination process starts from the back of the brain and works its way to the front. That means the prefrontal cortex, the area of the brain involved in decision-making, planning and self-control, is the last part to mature. It's not that teens don't have frontal-lobe capabilities but rather that their signals are not getting to the back of the brain fast enough to regulate their emotions. It's why risk-taking and impulsive behavior are more common among teens and young adults. "This is why peer pressure rules at this time of life," says Jensen. "It's why my teenage boys would come home without their textbook and realize at 8 p.m. that they have a test the next day. They don't have the fully developed capacity to think ahead at this time."

Although the development of the prefrontal cortex is the last step on the development

The teenage brain has lots of plasticity, which means it can change, adapt and respond to its environment.

checklist, teenagers undergo major changes in their limbic system—the area of the brain that controls emotions—at the onset of puberty, which is typically around the ages of 10 to 12. Doctors now believe that this mismatch in development of the impulse-control part of the brain and the hormone- and emotion-fueled part of the brain is what causes the risk-taking behaviors that are so common among teenagers. "The prefrontal cortex communicates with the brain's emotional centers through intricate connections," says B.J. Casey, the director of the Fundamentals of the Adolescent Brain Lab at Yale University. "In adults, these connections have been strengthening with experience and maturation, but during adolescence, the connections are not fully developed, so it's more difficult for a teenager to shut off these emotional systems."

This new understanding of the biology that underlies these behaviors can be helpful to both teenagers and their parents. Jensen and Casey stress the importance of setting examples of appropriate emotional responses and helping young people navigate difficult situations that are increasingly common among teens and adolescents. Whereas in the past, bullying was primarily reserved for the playground, today teens have access to technologies and social media that can make it easier to spread sinister information. Virtual interactions can be harder for parents or teachers to control, but there is an immense opening to help teens navigate the fallout. "As parents, we often want to protect our kids from failure or any emotional pain," says Casey. "But opportunities for learning from such experiences in the context of a loving and supportive family are key to helping the adolescent develop and use this ability as an adult."

Studies in recent years have also suggested that mental abilities like IQ are not set in stone. A 2011 study published in the journal

How the adolescent brain develops

From early childhood through the teen years to early adulthood, the brain is in a constant state of flux. Here, brain scans show how gray-matter density reduces over time as synapses are pruned during the process of maturation.

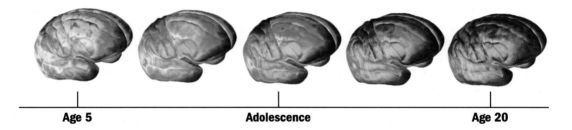

Age 5   **Adolescence**   **Age 20**

Nature measured the IQs of 33 teenagers—19 boys and 14 girls—in 2004, when they were 12 to 16 years old. The researchers then retested them in 2008 when they were 15 to 20 years old. The study authors discovered that IQ changed over time, improving for some people and deteriorating for others. Although members of the medical community often debate what an IQ test really measures, there is agreement that a person's score has implications for their learning and ability to perform tasks. "These changes are real, and they are reflected in the brain," Cathy Price, a neuroscientist at University College London, told *Science* magazine when the findings were released. "People's attitude is to decide early on that this is a clever kid and this is not a clever kid—but this suggests you can't make that assessment in the teenage years."

The realization that IQ can change underlines the importance of measuring mental engagement during the high school years—and cutting late bloomers some slack. The plasticity of the teenage brain means that it's never too late to get kids involved in learning. After-school activities, exercise and meditation can benefit brain circuitry. "Opportunities to find oneself and daring to meet challenges in science, education, within communities and among peers can have profound effects on our young people," says Casey.

The teen brain's rapidly growing connections carry some negative side effects. About 70% of mental illnesses, including anxiety, mood and eating disorders, and psychosis, appear in the teen years and early adulthood. The timing makes sense, since the prefrontal cortex and frontal lobes are implicated in the emergence of diseases like depression and schizophrenia.

Risks for health issues like addiction are also higher during this time period. "Addiction is simply a form of learning," says Jensen. "Addiction is repeated stimulation of the reward circuit in the brain, which is more mature than the frontal lobe at that point. The biology of teens' brains [makes them] more susceptible to the effects of substances and stress." Although the effects of cannabis use on the brain in adulthood are hotly debated, Jensen says research suggests that daily, chronic use during teenage years can interfere with development by having a sedative effect on the brain that can impair learning and memory.

"Teens can learn things harder, stronger, faster, and they can get addicted harder, stronger, faster," says Jensen. A 2016 study reported that the risk of addiction to opioids increased nearly 40% among young people ages 18 to 25 from 2002 to 2014.

Even with those risks, there's plenty that communities can do to set up teenagers and adolescents for success, including finding ways for them to de-stress and sleep. In the past few years, there's been a movement among local school districts to push back school start times, amid growing research that shows teens have a natural tendency to sleep in. When teens enter puberty, they undergo what's referred to as a sleep-phase delay. Teenagers' internal biological clocks shift forward, and they start having trouble falling asleep before 11 p.m. and waking up before 8 a.m. Research has linked lack of sleep among adolescents and teens to higher rates of chronic diseases like obesity and Type 2 diabetes, more caffeine use, poor impulse control, lower levels of motivation, impaired attention and memory, and more. The new science has led groups like the American Academy of Pediatrics to push for high schools to delay their start times so that students get more sleep each night.

"There's new knowledge that the wiring of emotional centers to the frontal lobes of the brain continues well into adolescence, and we can see that a lot of that wiring is taking place during sleep," says Mary Carskadon, a professor of psychiatry and human behavior at Brown University. "Emerging science suggests sleep may play an even more important role than we thought in terms of brain development."

Despite the knowledge that sleep is critical

Jay Giedd, a professor of psychiatry at the University of California, San Diego, studies brain changes.

for healthy brains, in the U.S., more than 4 in 5 middle and high schools begin at or before 8:30 a.m. Still, "it feels like we are reaching a tipping point, where sleep is now being conveyed as a serious and urgent public health matter," says Carskadon.

What's become increasingly clear is that the dramatic changes in brain biology mean the teenage years are full of opportunity and vulnerability, says Jay Giedd, a professor of psychiatry at the University of California, San Diego, who has been studying brain changes among twins for years. "It's a time of phenomenal leaps in our creativity and cognitive abilities," he says. "This seeming paradox of adolescence is not a coincidence. Both the leaps in ability and the vulnerabilities to illness are related to the human adolescent brain's remarkable ability to change."

Teaching young people about the complexities of their brains can go a long way. Jensen says she often receives thank-you notes from students after speaking about her research at high schools. "Teenagers are looking to understand themselves," she says. "It's great to have some explanations about why you did that stupid thing in front of your friends. I think talking about this gives them more insight."

There may be no way to prevent the uncertainty that comes from being a teenager, but there are ways to take advantage of those critical years. For Jensen, she developed go-to advice for her own sons and their peers: "Mind your brain now, and it will mind you later."

Linking Energy Drinks and TBIs

TEENS WHO OFTEN CONSUME THE DRINKS HAVE HIGHER RATES OF MAJOR BRAIN INJURIES

BY ALEXANDRA SIFFERLIN

In a 2015 study, researchers found that teens who reported having a traumatic brain injury (TBI) in the past year were seven times as likely to report drinking at least five energy drinks in the previous week as teens who did not have a TBI.

The report, published in the online journal *PLOS One*, looked at 2013 survey information from 10,272 students ages 11 to 20. Teens who experienced a TBI in the past 12 months were at least twice as likely to report drinking energy drinks mixed with alcohol. In addition, teens who got a TBI while playing team sports like hockey had double the likelihood of drinking energy drinks in the past year, compared with teens who suffered a TBI from other injuries such as fights or a car accident.

"We think the common denominator between traumatic brain injuries and energy drinks is sports," says study author Gabriela Ilie of the division of Neurosurgery and Injury Prevention Research Office at Toronto's St. Michael's Hospital. "Marketing campaigns for energy drinks usually are carefully crafted to include sponsorship of events that are very appealing to this age group, like snowboarding."

The reported use of energy drinks and alcohol among young people is of special concern, the study authors say. Prior research has suggested that caffeine can mask the effects of alcohol, making it more difficult for a person to determine when they should stop drinking.

"Mix [the energy drinks] with alcohol, and suddenly the effects of energy drinks alone pale in comparison to the physical and emotional risks posed by this mixture to a developing brain," says Ilie. "Let us keep in mind that our brain doesn't stop developing until mid-20s or even early 30s."

The researchers cannot draw a causal link between energy drinks and TBIs from their data. Ilie says the effects of energy drinks on a healthy brain are still very little understood and that more research is needed to understand the connection.

As TIME has previously reported, data indicates that about 50% of adolescents consume energy drinks and 31% do so on a regular basis. Young people appear to increasingly choose energy drinks over soda, and the U.S. energy-drink market is projected to grow more than 11% by 2019, to $26.6 billion in annual revenue.

"Suggesting that drinking energy drinks in some way uniquely contributes to this or any other injury is counter to the facts," the American Beverage Association, a trade group that represents the beverage industry, told TIME in a comment on the study.

"In fact, this study does not and cannot show a causal link between energy drinks and any adverse health outcome. Importantly, just this year the European Food Safety Authority (EFSA) once again confirmed the safety of energy drinks and their ingredients after an extensive review." Energy drinks are non-alcoholic beverages, says the trade group, which also notes that when it comes to caffeine, most mainstream energy drinks contain less than and sometimes only half as much as a similar-size cup of many specialty coffees.

"Until we better understand what the effects of these drinks are, we need to be vigilant and discourage the association between energy drinks and sports," says Ilie. "Surely there has to be another way to promote these drinks without the risk of harmful effects on teens."

Beating Teenage Depression

TODAY'S TEENS ARE UNDER INCREASING STRAIN FROM SOCIAL MEDIA AND THE PRESSURE TO BE PERFECT

BY SUSANNA SCHROBSDORFF

he first time Faith-Ann Bishop cut herself, she was in eighth grade. It was 2 in the morning, and as her parents slept, she sat on the edge of the tub at her home outside Bangor, Maine, with a metal clip from a pen in her hand. Then she sliced into the soft skin near her ribs. There was blood—and a sense of deep relief. "It makes the world very quiet for a few seconds," says Faith-Ann. "For a while I didn't want to stop, because it was my only coping mechanism. I hadn't learned any other way."

The pain of the superficial wound was a momentary escape from the anxiety she was fighting constantly, about grades, about her future, about relationships, about everything. Many days she felt ill before school. Sometimes she'd throw up; other times she'd stay home. "It was like asking me to climb Mount Everest in high heels," she says.

It would be three years before Faith-Ann, now 21 and a film student in Los Angeles, told her parents about the depth of her distress. She hid the marks on her torso and arms and hid the sadness she couldn't explain and didn't feel was justified. On paper, she had a good life. She loved her parents and knew they'd be supportive if she asked for help. She just couldn't bear seeing the worry on their faces.

Alison Heyland, seen at her home in Maine, was part of a group that made a film to raise awareness about depression, anxiety and self-harm.

For Faith-Ann, cutting was a secret, compulsive manifestation of the depression and anxiety that she and millions of teenagers in the U.S. are struggling with. Self-harm, which some experts say is on the rise, is perhaps the most disturbing symptom of a broader psychological problem: a spectrum of angst that plagues 21st-century teens.

Adolescents today have a reputation for being more fragile, less resilient and more overwhelmed than their parents were when they were growing up. Sometimes they're called spoiled or coddled or helicoptered. But a closer look paints a far more heartbreaking portrait of why young people are suffering. Anxiety and depression in high school kids have been on the rise since 2012 after several years of stability. It's a phenomenon that cuts across all demographics—suburban, urban and rural; those who are college-bound and those who aren't. Family financial stress can exacerbate these issues, and studies show that girls are more at risk than boys.

In 2015, about 3 million teens ages 12 to 17 had had at least one major depressive episode in the past year, according to the Department of Health and Human Services. More than 2 million report experiencing depression that impairs their daily function. About 30% of girls and 20% of boys—totaling 6.3 million teens—have had an anxiety disorder, according to data from the National Institute of Mental Health.

Experts suspect that these statistics are on the low end of what's really happening, since many people do not seek help for anxiety and depression. A 2015 report from the Child Mind Institute found that only about 20% of young people with a diagnosable anxiety disorder get treatment. It's also hard to quantify behaviors related to depression and anxiety, like nonsuicidal self-harm, because they are deliberately secretive.

Still, the number of distressed young people is on the rise, experts say, and they are trying to figure out how best to help. Teen minds have always craved stimulation, and their emotional reactions are by nature urgent and sometimes debilitating. The biggest variable, then, is the climate in which teens navigate this stage of development.

Anxiety and depression in high school kids have been on the rise since 2012 after years of stability.

They are the post-9/11 generation, raised in an era of economic and national insecurity. They've never known a time when terrorism and school shootings weren't the norm. They grew up watching their parents weather a severe recession, and, perhaps most important, they hit puberty at a time when technology and social media were transforming society.

"If you wanted to create an environment to churn out really angsty people, we've done it," says Janis Whitlock, the director of the Cornell Research Program on Self-Injury and Recovery. Sure, parental micromanaging can be a factor, as can school stress, but Whitlock doesn't think those things are the main drivers of this epidemic. "It's that they're in a cauldron of stimulus they can't get away from, or don't want to get away from, or don't know how to get away from," she says.

In my dozens of conversations with teens, parents, clinicians and school counselors across the country, there was a pervasive sense that being a teenager today is a draining full-time job that includes doing schoolwork, managing a social-media identity, and fretting about career, climate change, sexism, racism—you name it. Every fight or slight is documented online for hours or days after the incident. It's exhausting.

It's hard for many adults to understand how much of teenagers' emotional life is lived within the small screens on their phones, but a CNN special report in 2015 conducted with researchers at the University of California, Davis, and the University of Texas at Dallas examined the social-media use of more than 200 13-year-olds. Their analysis found that "there is no firm line between their real and online worlds," according to the researchers.

That hyperconnectedness now extends everywhere, engulfing even rural teens in a national thicket of internet drama. Daniel Champer, the director of school-based ser-

Phoebe Gariepy, a high school senior in Maine, learned to avoid places online that glorified sadness and self-destructive acts.

vices for Intermountain in Helena, Mont., says the one word he'd use to describe the kids in his state is "overexposed." Montana's kids may be in a big, sparsely populated state, but they are not isolated anymore. A suicide might happen on the other side of the state and the kids often know before the adults, says Champer. This makes it hard for counselors to help. And nearly 30% of the state's teens said they felt sad and hopeless almost every day for at least two weeks in a row, according to the 2015 Montana Youth Risk Behavior Survey. To address what they consider a cry for help from the state's teens, officials in Montana are working on expanding access to school-based and tele-based counseling.

School pressures also play a role, particularly with stress. Nora Carden, 17, in Brooklyn, got counseling for her anxiety, which became crushing as the college-application process ramped up. She'd fear getting an an-

swer wrong when a teacher called on her, and she often felt she was not qualified to be in a particular class. "I don't have pressure from my parents. I'm the one putting pressure on myself," she says.

Tommy La Guardia, a high-achieving 18-year-old senior in Kent, Wash., is the first college-bound kid in his family. He recently became a finalist for prestigious scholarships while working 10 to 15 hours a week at a Microsoft internship and helping to care for his younger brothers.

His mom, Catherine Moimoi, says he doesn't talk about the pressure he's under. They don't have a lot of resources, yet he manages everything himself, including college tours and applications. "He's a good kid. He never complains," she says. "But there are many nights I go to sleep wondering how he does it."

Conventional wisdom says kids today are oversupervised, prompting some parenting critics to look back fondly to the days of latchkey kids. But now, even though teens may be in the same room with their parents, they might also, thanks to their phones, be immersed in a painful emotional tangle with dozens of their classmates. Or they're looking at other people's lives on Instagram and feeling self-loathing (or worse). Or they're caught up in a discussion about suicide with a bunch of people on the other side of the country they've never even met via an app that most adults have never heard of.

In the CNN study, researchers found that even when parents try their best to monitor their children's Instagram, Twitter and Facebook feeds, they are likely unable to recognize the subtle slights and social exclusions that cause kids pain.

Finding disturbing things in a child's digital identity, or that they're self-harming, can stun some parents. "Every single week we have a girl who comes to the ER after some social-media rumor or incident has upset her [and then she cut herself]," says Fadi Haddad, a psychiatrist who helped start the child and adolescent psychiatric emergency department at Bellevue hospital in New York City, the first of its kind at a public hospital. Teens who end up there are often sent by administrators at their school. When Haddad calls the parents, they can be unaware of just how distressed their child is. According to Haddad, this includes parents who feel they're very involved in their children's lives: they're at every sports game, they supervise the homework, they're part of the school community.

For some parents who discover, as Faith-Ann's parents, Bret and Tammy Bishop, did a few years ago, that their child has been severely depressed, anxiety-ridden or self-harming for years, it's a shock laden with guilt.

Bret says Faith-Ann had been making cuts on her legs and ribs for three years before she got the courage to tell her parents. "You wonder, What could I have done better?" he says. Looking back, he realizes that he was distracted too much of the time.

Depression by the numbers

3 million

Adolescents ages 12 to 17 in the U.S. who had at least one **major depressive episode*** in the past year. This number has increased over time.

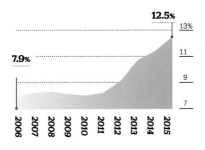

Girls are far more likely to experience depression

Female
19.5%

Male
5.8%

Anxiety by the numbers

6.3 million

Teens ages 13 to 18 who have had an **anxiety disorder.** That number represents 25% of the population in that age group in 2015.

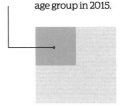

Boys are more likely to be anxious than depressed

Female
30.1%

Male
20.3%

*A MAJOR DEPRESSIVE EPISODE IS DEFINED AS A PERIOD OF TWO WEEKS OR LONGER DURING WHICH THERE IS EITHER A DEPRESSED MOOD OR LOSS OF INTEREST OR PLEASURE, AND AT LEAST FOUR OTHER SYMPTOMS THAT REFLECT A CHANGE IN FUNCTIONING, LIKE PROBLEMS WITH SLEEP, EATING, ENERGY, CONCENTRATION OR SELF-IMAGE. SOURCE: U.S. DEPARTMENT OF HEALTH AND HUMAN SERVICES

"Even for us as adults, you're never away from work now. Before, there wasn't anything to worry about till I got back on Monday. But now it's always on your phone. Sometimes when you're home, you're not home," Bret says.

When Bret and Tammy joined a group for parents of kids with depression, he discovered that there were many girls and some boys who were also depressed and hurting themselves—and that few parents had any idea of what was going on.

Tammy says she wishes she'd followed her gut and taken Faith-Ann for counseling earlier. "I knew something was wrong, and I couldn't figure it out," she says.

Self-harm is certainly not universal among kids with depression and anxiety, but it does appear to be the signature symptom of this generation's mental-health difficulties. All of the nearly two dozen teens I spoke with for this story knew someone who had engaged in self-harm or had done it themselves. It's hard to quantify the behavior, but its impact is easier to monitor: a Seattle Children's Hospital study that tracked hashtags people use on Instagram to talk about self-harm found a dramatic increase in their use in the past two years. Researchers got 1.7 million search results for "#selfharmmm" in 2014; by 2015 the number was more than 2.4 million.

Although girls appear more likely to engage in this behavior, boys are not immune: as many as 30% to 40% of those who've ever self-injured are male.

The academic study of this behavior is nascent, but researchers are developing a deeper understanding of how physical pain may relieve the psychological pain of some people who practice it. That knowledge may help experts better understand why it can be hard for some people to stop self-harming once they start. Whitlock, the director of the self-injury research program at Cornell, explains that studies are pretty consistent in showing that people who injure themselves do it to cope with anxiety or depression.

It's hard to know why self-harm has surfaced at this time, and it's possible we're just more aware of it now because we live in a world where we're more aware of everything.

Whitlock thinks there's a cultural element to it. Starting in the late 1990s, the body became a kind of billboard for self-expression—that's when tattoos and piercings went mainstream. "As that was starting to happen, the idea of etching your emotional pain into your body was not a big step from the body as a canvas as an idea," she says.

The idea that self-harm is tied to how we see the human body tracks with what many teens told me when I interviewed them. As Faith-Ann describes it, "A lot of value is put on our physical beauty now. All of our friends are Photoshopping their own photos—it's hard to escape that need to be perfect." Before the dawn of social media, the disorders that seemed to be the quintessential reflection of those same societal pressures were anorexia and bulimia—which are still serious concerns.

Whitlock says there are two common experiences that people have with self-harm. There are those who feel disconnected or numb. "They don't feel real, and there's something about pain and blood that brings them into their body," she says.

On the other end of the spectrum are people who feel an overwhelming amount of emotion, says Whitlock. "If you asked them to describe those emotions on a scale of 1 to 10, they would say 10, while you or I might rate the same experience as a 6 or 7. They need to discharge those feelings somehow, and injury becomes their way," she explains.

The research on what happens in the brain and body when someone cuts is still emerging. Scientists want to better understand how self-harm engages the endogenous opioid system—which is involved in the pain response in the brain—and what happens if and when it does.

Some of the treatments for self-harm are similar to those for addiction, particularly in the focus on identifying underlying psychological issues—what's causing the anxiety and depression in the first place—and then teaching healthy ways to cope. Similarly, those who want to stop need a strong level of internal motivation.

"You're not going to stop for somebody else," explains Phoebe, a teenager from Arundel, Maine, who self-harmed. Even thinking about how upset her mother was about the activity wasn't enough. "I tried making pacts with friends. But it doesn't work. You have to figure it out for yourself. You have to make the choice."

Eventually, Phoebe steered herself out of the dark, destructive corners of the internet that reinforced her habit by romanticizing and validating her pain. She's now into holistic healing and looks at positive sites populated by people she calls "happy hippies."

Faith-Ann remembers the day her mother, Tammy, noticed the scars on her arms and realized what they were. By then she was a junior in high school. "I normally cut in places you couldn't see, but I had messed up and I had a cut on my wrists. I lifted my arm to move my hair, and she saw it. It was scary because the cuts were in a place that people associate with suicide." That was not what she was attempting, however.

"If she'd asked me before that if I was cutting, I would have said no. I wouldn't have wanted to put that pain on her," says Faith-Ann. But that night she said, "Yes, I am cutting, and I want to stop." Tammy cried for a bit, but they moved on. She didn't ask why; she didn't freak out; she just asked what she could do to help. "That was the exact right thing to do," says Faith-Ann.

The family got counseling after that. Her parents learned that they weren't alone. And Faith-Ann learned breathing techniques to calm herself physically and ways to talk to herself positively. Recovery didn't happen all at once. There were relapses, sometimes over tiny things. But the Bishops were on the right road.

One of the most powerful things Faith-Ann did to escape the cycle of anxiety, depression and self-harm was to channel her feelings into something creative. As part of the Project Aware teen program in Maine, she wrote and directed a short film about anxiety and depression in teens called *The Road Back*. More than 30 kids worked on the project, and they became a support system for one another as she continued to heal.

Bellevue's Fadi Haddad says that for parents who find out their children are depressed or hurting themselves, the best response is

Faith-Ann Bishop had severe depression in high school. Now she's a film student in Los Angeles.

first to validate their feelings. Don't get angry or talk about taking away their computers. "Say, 'I'm sorry you're in pain. I'm here for you,'" he says.

This straightforward acknowledgment of their struggles takes away any judgment, which is critical since mental-health issues are still heavily stigmatized. No adolescent wants to be seen as flawed or vulnerable, and for parents, the idea that their child has debilitating depression or anxiety or is self-harming can feel like a failure on their part.

Faith-Ann still struggles at times with the weight of depression and anxiety. "It's a condition that's not going to totally disappear from my life," she says over the phone

from Los Angeles, where she's thriving at film school. "It's just learning how to deal in a healthy way—not self-harming, not lashing out at people."

Of course, Bret and Tammy Bishop still worry about her. They now live in Hampstead, N.C., and at first Bret didn't like the idea of Faith-Ann's going to school in California. If she was having trouble coping, he and Tammy were a long plane ride away. How can you forget that your child, someone you've dedicated years to keeping safe from the perils of the world, has deliberately hurt herself? "It's with you forever," says Tammy.

These days, she and Bret are proud of their daughter's independence and the new life she's created. But like a lot of parents who have feared for their child's health, they don't take the ordinary for granted anymore.

What parents should do

If you're worried about an adolescent and aren't sure what to do, heed the advice of Fadi Haddad, a psychiatrist and the co-author of *Helping Kids in Crisis*:

Talk about the real stuff

Sometimes conversations between parents and teens can be all about achievements, schedules and chores. Go beyond that. Find out what keeps them up at night, and ask, "What's the best part of your day?" Become attuned to their emotional world so that you understand what their dreams are, what they struggle with and how their life is going.

Pay attention, but don't smother them

Give teens space to grow and separate from you, but also watch for changes in behavior. Are they giving up activities they used to enjoy? Are they staying up all night or eating differently? Is your outgoing kid now withdrawn? If you're worried, say so. Show interest in their internal life without judgment.

Resist getting angry

When parents find out a teen has been hiding something or is having behavior issues, the response is often anger or punishment. Instead, find out what's going on. If a kid is acting out, say, "It seems like you're having trouble. I'm here to help. Tell me what's happening with you."

Don't put off getting help

If you're worried about an adolescent, talk to a school counselor, therapist or doctor. It's better to get help early than when trouble has firmly taken hold.

Treat the whole family

When a kid is in crisis, many times it's not enough to treat the child—you have to change the family dynamic. It's possible that something about the home environment was causing stress for the child, so be open to acknowledging that and getting family counseling if needed.

Teen Cliques

PARENTS NEED TO KNOW HOW TO HELP THEIR KIDS DEAL WITH THE PAIN OF SOCIAL EXCLUSION

BY LISA FREEDMAN

I t seems as if it happens overnight—and sometimes it does. One day your child feels like part of the gang; the next she's been elbowed out of the lunch table, excluded from a conversation at recess or left off the invitation list for a birthday party. When children are young, their friend groups usually consist of whomever their parents invite over for playdates, says Robert Faris, an associate professor of sociology at the University of California, Davis. As a result, these groups are often open and fluid. "Cliques, by contrast, are not orchestrated by parents," says Faris. "They are tightly knit—or seem so from the outside—and have strong boundaries." For one kid to be in a clique, another might get rejected from it.

Fortunately, amid all the whispering and ostracizing, seat saving and photo tagging, there is hope. With some understanding and smart strategies, you can help your kids get through the temptation to exclude, the pain of being left out and the many subtleties of intraclique relations, so they can come out happy(ish) on the other side. Cliques, in less catty forms, go back as far as humankind. "We come from a hunter-gatherer society," says Julie Paquette MacEvoy, an assistant professor

of psychology at Boston College who studies children's social and emotional development. "There was a greater chance of survival if you were part of a group. The urge to form cliques is evolutionarily ingrained."

By toddlerhood, this behavior starts to show up. A 2014 study published in *Psychological Science* showed that children as young as 2 will mimic their behavior to match that of their peers so they don't stand out from the crowd. And not long after toddlerhood, we're able to pinpoint the person in our group with whom we're closest. "I don't think we ever stop using that label [best friend]," says Rosalind Wiseman, a parenting educator and the author of *Queen Bees and Wannabes*. Why are we so attached to it? "We need to have the sense that we matter. If we have a best friend, that means we count to someone."

And though children today certainly won't perish if they don't have a core group of buddies, there are benefits, such as a boost to self-esteem and a sense of belonging, says Wiseman. Also, it just feels good to be included. That's why it's so painful to be left out.

Your child may see ejection from a friend group as the worst thing that's ever happened to her—and she might be right. For some kids, it can be more painful than being rejected by a crush because the latter pain involves only one person. "When you're pushed out of a clique, that's an entire group of people who don't value you, care about you or want to hang out with you," says MacEvoy. Research shows that exclusion triggers activity in the same part of the brain that controls physical pain, says Judith V. Jordan, an assistant professor of psychiatry at Harvard Medical School.

What can you do? Take your child's grief seriously. Resist the urge to downplay it, even though you know clique trouble is a universal experience and we pretty much all survive. If the situation seems to demand it, ask teachers for help in making sure the exclusion isn't overt or cruel. At home, listen to your child's daily recaps—if she's willing to share—and empathize, says MacEvoy. Tell her you understand why she's so upset with what's happening and that you would be too. But don't go that extra step of disparaging or belittling

other kids. As much as it may feel good to both of you in the moment, it sets the wrong example and could make reconciliation difficult for your child later.

To help make the next day at school—and the day after that, and so on—feel surmountable, ask your child if she would like to talk through hypothetical social scenarios. What should your child do if she has to eat lunch by herself? (Maybe she can read a book while she eats, or you two can talk about whom else she could approach.) What should she do if one of the girls says something mean to her? (Walk away.) For younger kids (up to around age 11 or 12), this exercise tends to feel empowering, says MacEvoy. Teenagers may find it cheesy; offer them an ear instead.

If there's potential for your child to patch things up or make amends, discuss the reasons for the exclusion in the first place. "Often it involves a member of the opposite sex—especially in adolescence—or just sheer jealousy," says MacEvoy. If your child offended just one member of her clique (and the rest of the girls are excluding her as an act of solidarity), encourage your kid to talk to the person with whom there's a real problem. If they can make up, it may be possible for the whole group to get back together, albeit with a bit of tension in the ranks.

Two types of dominant kids typically emerge during middle school: one who is positive and fun to be around, and another who is influential but also manipulative, says Brett Laursen, a professor of psychology at Florida Atlantic University. If your child hangs out with a manipulative leader, she may feel demeaned fairly frequently. What helps: emphasizing the importance of thinking for herself and being her own person, not merely the sidekick of a bossy pal. "Have conversations about when it's OK to give in and when it's not," says MacEvoy. For example, it's fine to let the group's leader decide which movie to watch if you don't care, but it's not OK for the queen bee to determine on her own who's invited to go to the movie. If you happen to have a child who's the leader of her clique, you can help her cultivate empathy by regularly asking her how her friends are feeling and doing.

When a group has truly caused pain—or formally ousted your child—she may have no choice but to leave it behind and seek out new friends. If she's feeling intimidated (and who wouldn't be?), talk about trying to make just one new friend rather than entering a whole new clique. Think about it: there's a world of difference between eating lunch alone and eating lunch across from someone else. Having additional friends is great too, but children are much less lonely when they have even one supportive friend, says Steven R. Asher, a professor of psychology and neuroscience at Duke University. It's ultimately up to your child to find this new buddy (or buddies), but you can lay the groundwork. Nudge her toward a club, a sport, a volunteer activity or even an after-school job where she can meet peers. And take heart in the knowledge that this lonely state isn't forever. Faris and his colleagues conducted a study in which they asked kids in the eighth through 12th grades to name their best friends every few weeks. "We found a shocking amount of turnover," he says. In other words: your child may feel excluded on Friday, but that doesn't mean she'll still be on the outs come Monday morning.

Yes and no. Boys and girls both seethe and gossip and experience betrayal and rejection. "But boys don't challenge the social hierarchy the way girls do," says Wiseman, the parenting educator. When boys feud, their social rankings usually get reinforced in the end. After the fight, "the boys go back to what was before," she says. Girls, on the other hand, take out their anger (or insecurity) by morphing the makeup of their friend groups. This form of fighting—in which the goal is to harm the other person's social status and relationships—is called relational aggression. The process can last for weeks or months and almost always involves manipulation and exclusion. Ouch.

Handling adult cliques

The PTA. Yoga class. The office lunchroom. Adult cliques are everywhere, and although these grown-up groupings usually aren't as cruel as younger iterations, they can still leave people feeling hurt. Here are three ways to fight the tendency and be a role model to your kids.

MAKE SMALL TALK

If you sit with the same moms at every soccer game, you may send the message that you're not interested in getting to know other parents, whether or not that's true. So why not invite someone on the bleacher below into a conversation? Offer a casual opening, like "I don't know. What do you think, Wendy? Amanda says that the hurricane forecast is just hype." Or strike up a conversation after the game in the parking lot. It will be quick and painless.

BE THOUGHTFUL

You don't have to be best buds with every woman in the office, but you do have to be nice. If you go on a latte run, consider bringing back a drink for a co-worker who's out of your circle, suggests Tasha R. Howe, a professor of psychology at Humboldt State University. Little gestures of kindness go far.

RESIST GOSSIP

It's hurtful to the targeted party, and it also reflects negatively on you. "Gossip often leaves a residue of doubt, uncertainty and insecurity," says Jordan, the psychiatry professor. The next time you're tempted to gossip, imagine your child sitting next to you and think of the example you would like to set.

1. Let them sleep in

It's not just a cliché. Teenagers really do sleep differently than the rest of us; they have a harder time going to bed early and a much, much easier time staying in bed the next morning. Teens have recently found unlikely allies in the many government and science groups that have come out in favor of letting them sleep in. Starting school after 8:30 a.m. can help sleep-deprived American teens (two thirds of them, to be exact) get the 8 to 10 hours they need for optimal health, according to the Centers for Disease Control and Prevention (CDC), the American Academy of Pediatrics and the American Academy of Sleep Medicine.

The groups concur that later start times mean students will be more focused during the school day, more alert while driving, and less likely to be absent or late. Schools are starting to take note, and some have begun pushing back the beginning of classes to later in the morning. But even if your teen's school has yet to catch on, encouraging him or her to go to sleep and wake up at the same time each day will help—as hard as that might be.

2. Split custody of the sex talk

When parents talk to their teens about sex, kids are more likely to have sex later and use contraception. But very few parents do it effectively, according to the American Academy of Pediatrics, which recently updated its sex-ed recommendations for the first time in 15 years.

One of the problems is that mothers are far likelier than fathers to talk with their kids about sex, and that doesn't appear to be the best way to reach sons. A new study of African-American fathers found that they were unsure of what to say to their sons about sex, and they weren't confident in their ability to talk about it.

The key is practice, says study author Tanya Coakley, an associate professor at the University of North Carolina at Greensboro department of social work. "The more times parents talk, the better they get at it." Create a welcoming atmosphere, be calm and nonjudgmental, and listen carefully, she advises. Parents should also

3. Don't introduce them to drinking

Many parents think it's better to be their child's alcohol sherpa than to let them discover drinking themselves. But scientists have found evidence for the opposite. Recent research finds that adolescents who were supplied alcohol by their parents were more likely to drink than those whose parents did not give them alcohol. (The good news: adolescents whose parents supplied alcohol didn't binge more than those who got booze elsewhere.) "The European approach to early introduction is romantically appealing," but it's not beneficial, says professor Richard Mattick of the National Drug and Alcohol Research Centre at the University of New South Wales in Australia. "There is no evidence that exposure to alcohol before the legal age of purchase decreases or moderates adolescent or early adult drinking, and good evidence that it increases consumption in teenage years and beyond."

---

make sure they're armed with the latest knowledge from the CDC about sexually transmitted infections but give a measured view about sex—not only the scary, negative parts.

4. Set a good digital example

Teens spend nine hours a day using screens, according to a recent report from Common Sense Media, a

nonprofit group focused on kids and technology. Turns out that's the same amount of time as parents. The same survey revealed that 78% of parents said they were "good technology role models" for their kids. To rein in your teen's use of cellphones, social media and texts, be aware of your own. Designate no-phone zones, such as the car, dinner table and bedroom.

5. Don't spy on them

It's tempting, but recent research shows that snooping on your teenagers isn't doing you, or them, any good. One study showed that the teenagers of parents who snooped weren't any more likely to be doing anything wrong than kids with parents who didn't. Instead, try talking frankly to your teen. A study in early 2017 found that kids were more likely to share information when their parents directly asked them questions, and more likely to withhold information when their parents snooped.

Best Books for Kids of All Ages

TIME and literary experts select classic literature for young people

25 of the Greatest Books for **Young Children**

Where the Wild Things Are
By Maurice Sendak. The adventure that has inspired generations of children to let out their inner monsters, showing how imagination allows for an escape from life's doldrums. It's also a moving testament to family love: when young Max returns from his reverie, his mother has saved him a hot dinner.

Frog and Toad
By Arnold Lobel. Two inseparable best friends keep each other company during all their adventures.

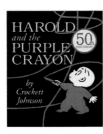

Harold and the Purple Crayon
By Crockett Johnson. A highly creative boy crafts entire worlds of his own devising, using only his trusty crayon.

Brave Irene
By William Steig. A dressmaker's daughter bravely ventures into a snowstorm to deliver the duchess her new gown in time for the ball.

Click, Clack, Moo
By Doreen Cronin; illustrations by Betsy Lewin. This story about farm animals sticking up for their rights wryly reveals the power of peaceful protest.

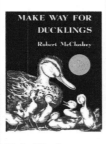

Make Way for Ducklings
By Robert McCloskey. A loving mother duck ferries her eight young ones through Boston.

Alexander and the Terrible, Horrible, No Good, Very Bad Day
By Judith Viorst; illustrations by Ray Cruz. Alexander's nonstop misfortunes pile up comically over the course of one outrageous day.

The Giving Tree
By Shel Silverstein. It's hard to imagine a story more poignant than the tale of a tree that gives its life for a boy who becomes increasingly self-centered as he grows up. It's been interpreted along environmentalist and religious lines, but all can agree on its underlying beauty.

Corduroy
By Don Freeman. In the middle of the night, a toy bear comes to life and hops off the shelf to replace his missing button.

Don't Let the Pigeon Drive the Bus!
By Mo Willems. One stubborn pigeon refuses to give up on his birdbrained dream of driving a vehicle.

Madeline
By Ludwig Bemelmans. A spunky French girl navigates boarding school and the removal of her appendix with confidence and poise.

I Want My Hat Back
By Jon Klassen. The witty account of a bear seeking out his lost hat; the illustrations are studded with subtle clues.

The Story of Ferdinand
By Munro Leaf; illustrations by Robert Lawson. Contrary to the stereotype of his species, Ferdinand is a calm, peaceful bull who would rather smell flowers than fight.

The Snowy Day
By Ezra Jack Keats. The journey of Peter through a snowbound New York City made for a milestone: as a successful children's story focused on a black protagonist, it broke down barriers many white editors may have never noticed. But Keats's book is memorable, too, for the sheer beauty of its collage illustrations.

Miss Rumphius
By Barbara Cooney. The story of a woman who spread flower seeds everywhere she went, filling Maine with blossoms.

The Lorax
By Dr. Seuss. Seuss takes on serious subject matter without compromising his playful style in this environmentalist fable.

Little Bear
By Else Holmelund Minarik; illustrations by Maurice Sendak. Minarik wrote these stories, the first of which conveys a young cub's yearning for his absent father, but it's Sendak's illustrations that catch the eye and allow for endless imaginings of life among woodland critters.

Blueberries for Sal
By Robert McCloskey. The block-printed illustrations show just how similar families of different species can be, as child Sal and a baby bear covet Maine blueberries on a berry hunt with their respective mothers. It's an instructive read for any kid who's ever felt a bit like a wild animal.

Owl Moon
By Jane Yolen; illustrations by John Schoenherr. Many young bird-watchers likely owe their passion to this wonderful story of a father-daughter trip to search for the elusive great horned owl.

25 of the Greatest Books for **Young Adults**

Little House on the Prairie
By Laura Ingalls Wilder. The books that spawned a literary and television franchise were based on Wilder's own experience growing up in the Midwest in the late 19th century.

The Chronicles of Narnia
By C.S. Lewis. The siblings Peter, Susan, Edmund and Lucy enter the magical world of Narnia, where they are charged with saving the realm from the evil White Witch.

Wonder
By R.J. Palacio. August Pullman, who has a rare facial deformity, decides to attend Beecher Prep for middle school, but he is forced to overcome bullying from some of his peers.

Olivia
By Ian Falconer. Charcoal illustrations splashed with red enrich a funny narrative about a confident little pig.

Where the Sidewalk Ends
By Shel Silverstein. Silverstein wasn't just good at tales of goofy self-sacrifice. His poems have spoken to kids' concerns and sparked their imaginations for decades. Any child who's ever fantasized about playing "tug o' war" instead of tug-of-war will find a kindred spirit here.

The True Story of the Three Little Pigs
By Jon Scieszka; illustrations by Lane Smith. This ironic, witty book, which revises the story of the pigs as an exculpatory memoir by the wolf—who claims he's not so big and bad at all!—is a welcome corrective to more saccharine tales. It also introduces young readers to the notion of dueling perspectives.

Anno's Journey
By Mitsumasa Anno. This visual feast doesn't need a single word to showcase the beauty of northern Europe.

Tuesday
By David Wiesner. Who needs text? Not this illustrator, who also "wrote" the few words that make up his tale. His watercolors show flying frogs on a surreal adventure. Reading is fundamental, but here the pictures do almost all the talking.

Goodnight Moon
By Margaret Wise Brown; illustrations by Clement Hurd. Somewhere a child is being put to sleep right now to Brown's soothing cadences. The lines may be etched in every parent's memory, but Hurd's illustrations, with their quirky hidden jokes, provide amusement on the thousandth reading.

The Sword in the Stone
By T.H. White. White gives the untold story of the legendary King Arthur's childhood and his training under the wizard Merlyn in this 1938 classic, the first book in the tetralogy *The Once and Future King.*

The Curious Incident of the Dog in the Night-Time
By Mark Haddon. A boy with autism investigates the murder of a neighbor's dog and in so doing explores life from an outsider's perspective.

Looking for Alaska
By John Green. Miles Halter attends boarding school in Alabama for his junior year, where he navigates the confusing social scene and falls in love with a girl named Alaska.

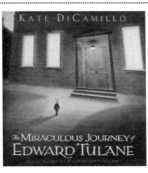

The Miraculous Journey of Edward Tulane
By Kate DiCamillo; illustrations by Bagram Ibatoulline. A doll rabbit's misfortune-plagued journey from owner to owner teaches him to care for and love others.

Anne of Green Gables
By L.M. Montgomery. Young, spirited Anne moves in with foster parents and adapts to her new home in Prince Edward Island.

25 of the Greatest Books for **Young Adults**

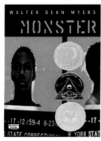

Monster
By Walter Dean Myers. A fictional account of an African-American teen on trial for felony murder in New York, written in a mix of journal entries and a third-person screenplay.

Roll of Thunder, Hear My Cry
By Mildred D. Taylor. A black family in the Depression-era American South grapples with racism.

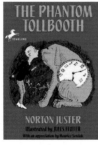

The Phantom Tollbooth
By Norton Juster; illustrations by Jules Feiffer. In a witty, sharp fairy tale that illuminates language and mathematics through a picaresque story of adventure in the Kingdom of Wisdom, Feiffer's whimsical drawings do as much as Juster's plain-language interpolations of complex ideas to carry readers through Digitopolis and the Mountains of Ignorance.

The Golden Compass
By Philip Pullman. Young Lyra Belacqua leads a battle in the Arctic to save children who were kidnapped and severed from their animal soul mates in this fantastical tale.

Holes
By Louis Sachar. A story of a family curse, fancy sneakers and poisonous lizards moves forward and backward through time, telling of how Stanley Yelnats IV ended up in a juvenile prison camp.

Charlotte's Web
By E.B. White; illustrations by Garth Williams. Readers are still drawn to the simplicity of arachnid Charlotte's devotion to her pig pal Wilbur. E.B. White's 1952 novel remains timeless for its enduring meditation on the power of friendship—and the power of good writing.

The Absolutely True Diary of a Part-Time Indian
By Sherman Alexie; illustrations by Ellen Forney. A coming-of-age novel illuminates family and heritage through Arnold Spirit Jr., torn between his life on a reservation and his largely white high school. This novel of self-discovery speaks to young readers everywhere.

The Diary of a Young Girl
By Anne Frank. Frank's poignant and relatable musings while hiding under Nazi occupation capture the tragedy of the Nazi regime.

From the Mixed-Up Files of Mrs. Basil E. Frankweiler
By E.L. Konigsburg. Claudia Kincaid, a precocious sixth-grader, and her 9-year-old brother Jamie run away from home and head for the Metropolitan Museum of Art, where they explore the exhibits and experience the majesty of great art.

The Giver
By Lois Lowry. This tale of self-discovery in a dystopian society has a memorable central character, Jonas, and an unforgettable message—that pain and trauma have an important place in individual lives and in society.

Harry Potter
By J.K. Rowling. What more can be said about this iconic franchise? How about this: a decade after the final volume was published, readers young and old still go crazy at the slightest rumor of a new Potter story.

Are You There God? It's Me, Margaret.
By Judy Blume. Twelve-year-old Margaret, whose mother is Christian and father Jewish, explores her heritage while overcoming the general social and personal challenges of a preteen girl.

Matilda
By Roald Dahl; illustrations by Quentin Blake. Poor Matilda feels thwarted and ignored by her family—a sense that many preteens share. They don't share her magical powers, but that's the appeal of this escapist frolic.

The Book Thief
By Marcus Zusak. For many readers, this novel provides their first contemplation of the Holocaust. Although terror surrounds Liesel, a young German girl, so too do friendship, love and charity—redeeming lights in the darkness.

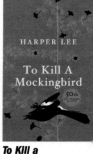

To Kill a Mockingbird
By Harper Lee. Scout Finch grows up in the racially charged Depression-era South, where her father, the lawyer Atticus Finch, is defending a black man accused of raping a young white woman.

The Outsiders
By S.E. Hinton. This coming-of-age novel offers proof that even the youngest writer can provide insight. Her striking look at Ponyboy and gang life in the 1960s has resonated for decades.

A Wrinkle in Time
By Madeleine L'Engle. This surrealist adventure has provided generations of children with their first-ever mind-blowing experiences, as Meg travels across the fifth dimension in search of her father.

TIME

Editor Nancy Gibbs
Creative Director D.W. Pine
Director of Photography Kira Pollack

The Science of Childhood

Editor Bryan Walsh
Designer D.W. Pine
Writers David Bjerklie, Lisa Freedman, Alison Gopnik, Kathleen Ann Harper, Jeffrey Kluger, Melissa Locker, Belinda Luscombe, Mandy Oaklander, Siobhan O'Connor, Ingela Ratledge, Bonnie Rochman, Joanne Ruthsatz, Susanna Schrobsdorff, Alexandra Sifferlin, Juliana Sohn, Kimberly Stephens, William Paul White
Photo Editor Dot McMahon
Copy Editor Joseph McCombs
Reporter David Bjerklie
Editorial Production David Sloan

TIME INC. BOOKS
Publisher Margot Schupf
Vice President, Finance Cateryn Kiernan
Vice President, Marketing Jeremy Biloon
Executive Director, Marketing Services Carol Pittard
Director, Brand Marketing Jean Kennedy
Sales Director Christi Crowley
Associate Director, Finance Jill Earyes
Associate Director, Brand Marketing Bryan Christian
Assistant General Counsel Andrew Goldberg
Assistant Director, Production Susan Chodakiewicz
Senior Manager, Finance Ashley Petrasovic
Brand Manager Katherine Barnet
Prepress Manager Alex Voznesenskiy
Project Manager Hillary Leary

Editorial Director Kostya Kennedy
Creative Director Gary Stewart
Director of Photography Christina Lieberman
Editorial Operations Director Jamie Roth Major
Senior Editor Alyssa Smith
Manager, Editorial Operations Gina Scauzillo
Associate Art Director Allie Adams
Assistant Art Director Anne-Michelle Gallero
Copy Chief Rina Bander
Assistant Editor Courtney Mifsud

Special thanks: Kristina Jutzi, Seniqua Koger, Kate Roncinske, Kristen Zwicker

Credits

"I guess that's what growing up is. Saying goodbye to a lot of things. Sometimes it's easy and sometimes it isn't. But it is all right."

—

Beverly Cleary